LATINO
CULTURE

LATINO CULTURE

A Dynamic Force in the Changing American Workplace

Nilda Chong AND *Francia Baez*

INTERCULTURAL PRESS

A Nicholas Brealey Publishing Company

YARMOUTH, ME • BOSTON • LONDON

First Published by Intercultural Press, a Nicholas Brealey Publishing Company, in 2005

Intercultural Press, Inc.
A Nicholas Brealey Publishing Company
PO Box 700
Yarmouth, Maine 04096 USA
Information: 1-888-BREALEY
Orders: 207-846-5168
Fax: 207-846-5181
www.interculturalpress.com

Nicholas Brealey Publishing
3-5 Spafield Street
London, EC1R 4QB, UK
Tel: +44-(0)-207-239-0360
Fax: +44-(0)-207-239-0370
www.nbrealey-books.com

© 2005 by Nilda Chong and Francia Baez

Printed in the United States of America

09 08 07 06 05   1 2 3 4 5

ISBN: 1-931930-13-9

Library of Congress Cataloging-in-Publication Data

Chong, Nilda.
   Latino culture : a dynamic force in the changing American workplace / Nilda Chong and Francia Baez.— 1st ed.
        p. cm.
   Includes bibliographical references and index.
   ISBN 1-931930-13-9
   1. Hispanic Americans—Employment. 2. Intercultural communication. I. Baez, Francia. II. Title.
   HD8081.H7C46 2005
   658.3'0089'68073—dc22

                                                            2005009299

Contents

To Kyn for countless words of wisdom.

To Manuel and Ana Palau, Vernon and Afroze Edwards, and Frances Saunders for their constant support and encouragement.

—Nilda Chong

To God, who, through my sister, Dr. Lourdes Baezconde-Garbanati, motivated me with this book to spread my wings and fly. I hope she and I can continue to fly together as in His name we fulfill the experiences of our lives. To my parents, Julio and Maia; to my husband, Cheo, and my children, Gabriela, Amelia, Andres, Rafael, and my nephew Alexander, who as Latinos growing up in the United States have been my inspiration. Thank you all for being part of my life.

—Francia Baez

Introduction

This book is written for mainstream employees, supervisors, and managers who work with Latinos. It is based on our combined experience of more than 40 years working as managers of Latinos both in the United States and in Latin America.

The purpose of the book is to provide information that will be helpful in developing an understanding of and sensitivity to the nuances of the Latino culture in the workplace and the ways it may affect an employee's behavior in common workplace situations. We hope that the illustrative vignettes presented in each chapter will highlight key behaviors and values shared by many individuals of Latino heritage living and working in the United States.

We consider individuals to be Latinos if they can trace their family origins to any of 21 different countries in Latin America. They span first to fourth generations; beyond that, the person has become almost entirely mainstream and therefore is outside the purview of this book. First-generation individuals—that is, Latino immigrants—have various levels of acculturation. Where possible, we discuss generational differences, especially when these differences may have an impact in the work environment. To accomplish our goal, we present here the most common shared values and characteristics of Latinos in the United States.

Most authors agree that the closer an individual is to the immigration experience, the greater the attachment to his or her cultural values. Thus, the more years that have passed since immigration, the greater the level of acculturation. Some authors have identified issues of selective acculturation among certain Latino groups. These groups retain some cultural values regardless of the number of years since immigration. As a result, some Latinos may behave as mainstream individuals at work but may act as Latinos at home. For example, a second-generation Latino supervisor, while at work, may speak only English and exhibit mainstream, individualistic behavior. At home, however, the same individual will speak Spanish and appreciate each joke-telling moment spent in the company of parents, siblings, cousins, aunts and uncles, and grandparents. In most cases, family traditions are treasured across generations of Latinos, especially when it comes to food preparation reserved for special holiday celebrations.

According to the U.S. Bureau of the Census, Latinos will represent close to 25 percent of the U.S. population by 2050. That means that one out of every four individuals living in the United States will have Latino ancestry. Your manager, your supervisor, your employees, your child's teacher, your hairdresser, your tailor—maybe even your spouse or your children's spouses—may be of Latino origin. The face of the Latino community is changing rapidly and evolving dramatically. Intermarriage among Latinos and between Latinos and members of other cultural groups will continue to define and redefine Latino physical and behavioral characteristics as they retain some or all their cultural values by 2050 and beyond.

A final comment is in order. Each Latino employee, supervisor, or manager is a unique individual, whose actions and reactions to work-related events may be tinted by personal factors such as academic attainment, work experience, upbringing, and personality, as well as by cultural background. There is no one-size-fits-all formula for facing the myriad of possible situations that may emerge in the workplace. Because our intent in writing this book is to share information, many discussions involve generalizations. Ultimately, though, every person is a unique individual, not a stereotype.

CHAPTER ONE

Who Are Latinos?

On Monday morning, you call your long-distance service provider and, after the automated greeting, you are given two options: *For English, press one; for Spanish, press two*. On Tuesday afternoon, you go to your bank to make a deposit, and you notice that the bank is decorated with colorful banners with messages in Spanish promoting credit cards, savings accounts, and loans. As you wait in line, you hear Spanish spoken all around you. Two days later, as you are going to work, a billboard with Latino faces and a soft drink advertising message in Spanish catches your attention.

Regardless of whether you are scanning to find a radio station, walking down the aisle of a grocery store, or just looking for a book in the library in many cities of the United States, it is not unusual to hear Spanish or to see Latinos. Why is this such a common experience? Because more than one in eight individuals living in the United States can trace his or her origins back to Mexico, Central America, South America, or the Spanish-speaking islands of the Caribbean.

In 2003, Latinos became the largest minority group in the United States, outnumbering African Americans and surpassing Asian Pacific Islanders. Almost 39 million Latinos—more than Canada's total population, which was estimated at 30 million in 2003—now live in the United States, representing more than 13 percent of the total U.S. population. Latinos' buying power will likely reach close to $1 trillion by 2007 and exceed African American buying power in 2008. Such projections capture the attention of businesses, radio and television networks, and print media, while they challenge advertising agencies' abilities to develop effective marketing strategies to reach this population (Hispanic Business 2003; Humphreys 2004).

Latinos currently have the highest rate of employment of any U.S. minority, and in five years their role in the American labor force will be even more prominent than it is now. Thus, understanding Latinos, their culture, and how they interact in the work environment may be crucial for organizations interested in attaining their business objectives. To assist in achieving that understanding, this chapter will provide a snapshot of the group.

DEMOGRAPHICS

There are at least four generations of Latinos living in the United States. Their median age is 26, with a higher proportion of young adults and children and fewer elderly than in the non-Latino population. It is common to hear immigrant Latinos indicate that when they die they want to be buried back home. Many use their savings to buy a house in their country of origin and move back when they retire.

LATINOS IN THE UNITED STATES: DEMOGRAPHICS

- *Age:* Thirty-four percent of Latinos are under the age of 18, 33 percent are between the ages of 25 and 44, and 14 percent are between 45 and 64.

- *Gender:* Fifty-one percent of Latinos are male; 49 percent are female.

- *Largest national groups:* The four largest groups are Mexicans (67 percent), Central Americans and South Americans (14 percent), Puerto Ricans (9 percent), and Cuban Americans (4 percent).

- *Geographic concentration:* Latinos are concentrated in California (31 percent), Texas (19 percent), New York (8 percent), and Florida (8 percent). In addition, significant numbers of Latinos live in Illinois, Arizona, New Jersey, New Mexico, Colorado, and Washington, DC.

- *Demographic projections:* By 2015, 25 percent of U.S. teenagers will be of Latino descent; by 2050, 25 percent of the U.S. population will be Latino.

There are no significant differences in Latinos' distribution by gender (Bernstein and Bergman 2003; Ramírez and de la Cruz 2002; Verdecia 2003). Two in five Latinos are foreign-born, with family origins in Mexico, Central America, South America, or the Spanish-speaking Caribbean islands (Ramírez and de la Cruz). Most Latinos live in the southern and western regions of the United States, and the majority prefer urban areas. They are more numerous in states that have borders with or are relatively accessible to Latin American countries, and where job opportunities are available, especially in the farming and construction industries (Bureau of the Census 1993b). Living in these states allows Latinos to be geographically closer to their families and to use their skills as farmers or construction workers while filling positions that are in high demand. Staying close to the family is important for Latinos of most age groups. Young, high-potential Latinos who work for global companies sometimes reject professional opportunities in Asia or Europe because they do not want to be so many hours away from aging parents or children studying in the U.S.

In the next 20 years, second-generation Latinos, the U.S.-born children of immigrant Latinos, will become the largest segment of the group. Currently, births outrank immigration in determining the growth of this population. Latina immigrants have the highest fertility rates of all groups in the country (Suro and Passel 2003). It has been projected that in the future the older, foreign-born population in the United States will consist mainly of individuals born in Latin America and Asia (He 2002).

Will Latino cultural factors alter the expected course of events? Some authors report that the family remains an essential cultural value even when immigrants have adjusted to a new country through the process of *acculturation*. Others have proposed that with future generations, the Latino value of *familism*, the extended family (grandparents, aunts, uncles, cousins, etc.), may change, especially as second-generation Latinos emerge as the predominant subgroup. Immigrants generally live in communities where they find a strong social support network that helps them provide a good life for their families. Their grown children, however, may move away in search of better jobs or may marry outside the community. Thus, the role of the Latino extended family may become less of a priority when compared with the need to have a secure job and to be able to support the nuclear family (parents and children).

HISPANIC OR LATINO?

In 1960, the U.S. Bureau of the Census created the term *Hispanic* to refer to people of Spanish ancestry (i.e., from Spain) and whose mother tongue was the Spanish language. Over the next three decades, people from the countries of Latin America continued to immigrate to the United States, with a significant influx of Central Americans in the 1980s. The latter group completed the mosaic of U.S. Latinos, and the five major sub-groups became more clearly defined as Mexican Americans, Cuban Americans, Puerto Ricans, Central Americans, and South Americans.

This prompted the Census Bureau to propose a revised definition of *Hispanic* in 1993, to refer to persons whose origins were Mexican, Puerto Rican, Cuban, Central or South American, or some other Hispanic origin. Latinos, however, appeared to resent the use of *Hispanic* by government agencies, preferring *Latino* because the latter term made reference to Latin America. The term *Latino* was officially established in 1997 when the Office of Management and Budget published recommendations for classification of federal race and ethnicity data indicating that the terms *Hispanic* and *Latino* were to be used interchangeably as of January 1, 2003 (Office of Management and Budget 1997).

Preference for one term over the other appears to have shifted in recent years, with much debate, as the composition of the group contin-ues to evolve dynamically. A recent survey revealed that almost all indi-viduals from Spanish-speaking backgrounds prefer to identify themselves by their country of origin. One study showed that 53 percent of respon-dents accepted both terms, while 34 percent preferred *Hispanic* and 13 percent leaned toward *Latino* (Suro et al. 2003).

We will use the term *Latino* in this book for two reasons. First, it has been the preferred term for many years, and it may be too early to settle on a definitive conclusion regarding the preferred terminology. Future reports may shed new light, given the dynamic changes currently taking place within the group. Second, both of us are immigrants from Latin America, and we strongly identify with the term *Latino*. We will continue to follow the debate closely as it evolves in the coming years.

LATINO OR LATINA?

Latino can be used generically to describe all people, both men and women, whose family origins are in Latin America. In some contexts, the word can also denote gender, with *Latino* referring to a male individual (plural, *Latinos*) and *Latina* to a female individual (plural, *Latinas*). In this book we will use *Latino* to refer to all individuals who are members of this community, regardless of gender, but we will use *Latina* as appropriate when referring to females only.

THE ROLE OF LATINOS IN THE U.S. ECONOMY

There are 16 million Latino men and women in the U.S. labor force. Their presence is prominent among service workers, laborers, operatives, office and clerical workers, and sales clerks. In particular, they are overrepresented in industries that have high fatality rates, such as construction and farming (Blassingame 2004; Cattan 1993; Repak 1993). Latinos' overrepresentation in these industries may reflect their level of education and their limited proficiency in the English language. Lack of understanding of preventive and safety measures at work may contribute to high fatality rates among Latinos.

Latinos currently hold only 1.1 percent of all executive-officer positions at the nation's top companies. Although they are still underrepresented, companies are increasingly interested in recruiting talented Latino candidates to fill managerial positions; they recognize that Latino managers will understand and interact effectively with Latino employees. Increase in access to education will likely create opportunities for second-generation Latinos to join the workforce and move into positions of increasing responsibility in the future (Bureau of the Census 2000; Dina

2003; Gómez 2004; HispanTelligence Report 2003b; Mundra, Moellmer, and Lopez-Aqueres 2003; Porter 2002; Thomas-Breitfeld 2003).

In March 2002, 22 percent of Latinos were employed in service occupations, compared with 12 percent of non-Hispanic whites. In contrast to non-Hispanic whites, Latinos were twice as likely to have low-wage jobs as operators and laborers, with only 14 percent holding managerial and professional positions. Central and South Americans were the most likely to work in service jobs, and Mexicans were the least likely to hold managerial and professional positions.

As of March 2002, 8 percent of Latinos over age 16 who were in the labor force were unemployed. Despite their current high unemployment rates, dramatic changes are likely to occur in the next two decades as increasing numbers of Latinos, following the trend of the last thirty years, attain higher levels of education, and as many of them are able to legalize their immigrant status. Latinos are projected to become more fully incorporated into the U.S. economy in the future, as the number of Latino workers will increase by 36 percent during this decade and will top 13 percent of the U.S. labor force by 2010 (Ramírez and de la Cruz; Thomas-Breitfeld).

Second-generation Latinos will gain prominence in the U.S. labor force between 2000 and 2020. According to projections (Ramírez and de la Cruz 2002), the Latino labor force will increase by 77 percent during these two decades, while the non-Latino labor force will grow by only 9 percent. It has been estimated that during this period there will be twice as many second-generation Latinos in schools as there are now, and three times the current number of Latinos in the labor force (Suro and Passel).

It is with an eye toward the challenges of these coming years that we embarked upon writing this book. The Latino work ethic is impressive; nonetheless, some Latinos' behaviors and attitudes in the workplace may reflect specific cultural values that have the potential to cause confusion and lead to miscommunication with non-Latino coworkers, supervisors, and supervisees who have limited knowledge of the Latino culture. Our goal is to increase opportunities to open the door to better communication and, consequently, to a more productive workforce.

Throughout the book, we offer vignettes illustrating workplace interactions involving Latino colleagues, managers, supervisors, and subordinates. We respectfully challenge you, our readers, to attempt to gain a deeper understanding of our Latino culture by placing yourself on both sides of the situations described in these vignettes.

Latino Diversity

While attending a conference recently, I (Nilda) was asked to regroup with other Latinos for a breakout session to discuss strategies for reaching Latinos in the United States. To everyone's surprise, the greatest challenge our group encountered was finding common ground to start the session. The seven participants included a Peruvian nurse who works as a university professor, a contractor of Mexican origin, a Colombian writer turned teacher, a restaurant owner from Argentina, a physician who emigrated from Cuba and works as a university researcher, a U.S.-born psychologist whose parents emigrated from the Dominican Republic, and a pharmacist from Puerto Rico. It was only because of our shared commitment to getting the work done successfully that we managed to launch our discussion. Latinos living in the United States share values and beliefs that set them apart from non-Latino whites, African Americans, Asian Pacific Islanders, and Native Americans. But they are also a highly diverse population, with clearly defined intragroup differences.

It is crucial to understand the issues that characterize each subgroup because using a generic approach to communicating with Latinos in the workplace may be an ineffective approach. For example, marked dissimilarities exist between individuals born in Latin America and Latinos born in the United States. Immigrant Latinos are a diverse group, with variations in their acculturation level and immigration status. Depending on their countries of origin, they tend to concentrate in different states and to differ in the level of education they have attained. They represent all races and at least four generations, as we will explain later in this chapter.

We will now look at six factors that we believe weigh heavily on cross-cultural communication situations involving many Latinos in the workplace: language, country of origin, generation, religion, race, and educational attainment.

LANGUAGE

Mainstream individuals who want to establish effective communication with Latinos should bear in mind that, for Latinos, language is as important as gestures and physical contact are. (We will discuss gestures in Chapter 4; the use of Spanish in the workplace will be presented in Chapter 6.)

Most first-generation Latinos speak Spanish, second-generation Latinos tend to be bilingual, and those of the third and fourth generations are likely to be English speakers. About 47 percent of Latinos are Spanish-dominant, 25 percent are English-dominant, and 28 percent are bilingual (Suro et al. 2002). An advertising industry study recently reported that 75 percent of all U.S. Latinos speak English well or very well and either are bilingual or use English exclusively (HispanTelligence 2003).

It is not uncommon to hear acculturated and second-generation Latinos speaking *Spanglish,* a conversational language that combines English words with Spanish or anglicized Spanish. For example, Mexicans may say, "I bought *la trocka* yesterday" ("I bought the truck yesterday"). Cuban Americans may say, "*Voy a mopear el* floor" ("I'm going to mop the floor"). The practice is becoming so widespread that several dictionaries exist as guides to Cuban Spanglish or Mexican American Spanish.

It is fair to say that the Spanish language unites Spanish-speaking Latinos. Still, the wide variety of accents, intonations, slang, and idioms attests to the diversity of the group. When interacting among themselves, immigrant Latinos are often able to recognize the speaker's region or country of origin on the basis of the use of specific idioms and accents. For example, Mexicans tend to use more idioms than do Central Americans, who generally speak at a fast pace and often run words together. Cubans and Puerto Ricans speak briskly and enunciate well, whereas

South Americans speak with almost musical intonations and often use a more sophisticated vocabulary, which may be a reflection of higher educational attainment. Being aware of these nuances may help mainstream Americans who know some Spanish to better understand their Latino peers at work.

It is also important to know that Latinos often use double meanings, in which one word or phrase idiomatically means another. When I (Francia) was living in Mexico, I remember panicking when a friend approached me and said, "Tomorrow we are having a party *en la casa de usted,*" meaning "in your house." He actually meant that he was having a party at his house but that he wanted me to consider his home as if it were my own. I thanked him, and then—not understanding what was going on—I turned to my husband to ask if he was organizing a party at our house without my knowledge.

Difficulties presented by the variations in the ways Latinos speak Spanish seem to have been overcome by the Latino media's use of "broadcast Spanish," a form of generic Spanish that is spoken without an identifiable accent and with few or no regional or national idiomatic expressions.

COUNTRY OF ORIGIN

Latinos can trace their origins to 21 different Spanish-speaking countries, collectively referred to as Latin America: Mexico, Guatemala, Nicaragua, Honduras, El Salvador, Costa Rica, Panamá, Colombia, Perú, Ecuador, Venezuela, Bolivia, Paraguay, Uruguay, Argentina, Chile, Puerto Rico, Dominican Republic, Cuba, Belize, and Brazil. Brazil is the only country included in Latin America where Portuguese, instead of Spanish, is spoken. Brazilians share many values with people from Spanish-speaking Latin American countries. Individuals from Spain are also included with Latinos.

Latinos of Mexican origin encompass the largest subgroup, currently an estimated 67 percent of all U.S. Latinos (Ramírez and de la Cruz 2002). Mexicans became the first Latino group in the United States as a result of the cession of Mexican lands to the U.S. in 1848 with the signing of the Treaty of Guadalupe Hidalgo. Under this treaty, Mexico ceded the land that is now California, Arizona, New Mexico, Utah, Nevada, and portions of other states. Latinos of Mexican origin are a diverse subgroup, ranging from mainstream to recent immigrants. For example, it would not be uncommon to meet a Mr. Steve Garcia, a bilingual, mainstream business executive born in Texas; a Mr. Jesús González, a landscape gardener who emigrated from Mexico to the U.S. six months ago and speaks only Spanish; or a Miss Mónica Hurtado, who came to the U.S. when she was two, has a graduate-level education, and is bilingual and bicultural.

Central Americans and Spanish-speaking South Americans are the second largest subgroup, encompassing 14.3 percent of all U.S. Latinos. In particular, many Nicaraguans and Salvadorans fled civil wars in their countries and were often denied political refugee status upon arriving in the United States. Being granted political asylum facilitates the process of finding a job, educating one's children, and ultimately becoming a U.S. citizen. Many of those who entered the country illegally later took advantage of a moratorium offered by the Immigration and Naturalization Service (INS) and legalized their status in the U.S. Although many Latinos who experienced war and civil unrest exhibit signs and symptoms of posttraumatic stress syndrome, most maintain a positive attitude toward work and life in the U.S. Many cannot return to their countries for political reasons, so they strive for higher education, seek increased responsibilities in the workplace, and encourage their children to reach higher levels of achievement. Their children, who generally immigrated when they were very young, are mostly bilingual and bicultural. María, a Nicaraguan clerk I (Nilda) met the other day at an office supplies store, shared with me that her husband works for a courier company and her two grown children, Marcos and Elizabeth, work as bank tellers. She proudly announced that they will be getting their college degrees next year. María's children, like many other Central Americans, work in service positions by day while going to school by night to get a college degree.

The influx of South Americans has been less significant in both absolute and relative numbers, although in recent years the number of

Argentinians, Colombians, and Venezuelans immigrating to the United States appears to be on the increase as a result of the economic and political crises in their countries. These immigrants are typically well educated, which helps to facilitate their incorporation into the workforce.

Puerto Ricans, the third largest Latino subgroup in the United States, represent 8.6 percent of all Latinos. As with most other immigrants, their motivation for moving to the U.S. is the search for a better life. Puerto Ricans have been entitled to U.S. citizenship since 1917, when Puerto Rico became a U.S. protectorate (Fernández 1991; Ramírez and de la Cruz). Many Puerto Ricans are bilingual and bicultural and are part of mainstream society, whereas others regularly travel back and forth between the island and the mainland to visit relatives.

Cubans are the least numerous subgroup. The first wave of Cubans who arrived in this country in the 1960s consisted mostly of educated middle- and upper-class families who fled Cuba in the "freedom flights" after Fidel Castro embraced communism. In contrast, the second wave of Cubans—often referred to as Marielitos because they left from the Port of Mariel—were less well educated and exhibited social and health problems uncommon in the earlier groups. The circumstances surrounding the Cuban immigration process have affected the lives of those who emigrated more than those of their U.S.-born children. For example, Eliseo and his wife, Noelia, who immigrated to the United States in the 1960s, are bilingual. Their food and music are Cuban, and they still long to go back someday, after Castro dies. Their children, Carlos and Lilia, were one and three years old, respectively, when they came to the U.S. with their parents. Although they understand their parents' culture, they are bilingual and identify strongly with mainstream U.S. culture. Carlos and Lilia have few memories of their childhood in Cuba and do not even consider returning to the island; for them, the U.S. is home.

It is worth mentioning here that some immigrants from Latin America are children of immigrants themselves. For example, Brazil and Perú had important Japanese migrations between 1899 and 1908. Argentina and Chile received a significant influx of Spanish, English, German, and Italian immigrants beginning in the late nineteenth century. Chinese immigrants have found their homes in many countries of Latin America as well.

In the workplace, Latinos who share the same country of origin tend to form groups. It is wise to be aware of the existence of such subgroups because, in a work environment where various subgroups are represented, some tension may develop as a result of intergroup differences. For example, a Latino recruiter may be faced with choosing between two equally qualified Latino job candidates. Most likely the recruiter may feel pressure to choose the applicant from his or her home country, as an expression of brotherhood or sisterhood.

Many mainstream Americans may assume that all Latinos are of Mexican origin. One of our Central American friends was once asked if she ate hot and spicy tacos and burritos at home every day before immigrating to California. The assumption was that she was of Mexican origin, when, in fact, she had learned to enjoy Mexican food only after coming to the United States. In her country of origin, Mexican restaurants are not as common as they are in the United States, especially in California.

GENERATION

In the workplace, issues of cross-cultural communication are more likely to occur with first-generation individuals than with those of the second or third generation, and such issues are likely to become even less common with the Pan-Latino generations of the future, reflecting intermarriage between Latinos from different subgroups, who will likely be members of the mainstream culture.

First-generation Latinos are those who were born in Latin America; second-generation individuals are, as we mentioned earlier, U.S.-born with at least one parent born in Latin America; and third-generation Latinos are the U.S.-born children of U.S.-born Latin American parents (Suro and Passel 2003). Recently, the concept of a one-and-a-half-generation Latino has been introduced to refer to individuals who emigrated from Latin America to the U.S. at an early age. Distinct issues separate this group from first- and second-generation Latinos. Given that the two largest subgroups, Mexicans and Central Americans, initiated immigration waves during different periods, it is estimated that there may be three or four generations of persons of Mexican origin in the United States and probably about two generations of Central Americans residing in the U.S.

First-generation immigrants tend to adhere to their cultural values and language as they make adjustments and experience the acculturation process. Some cultural values are consciously and voluntarily retained, while others are modified, often out of necessity, as immigrants adjust to their new country. With more time living in the United States, these immigrants, who generally came to this country as adults, often become incorporated into mainstream society (Domino and Acosta 1987). Although they will modify their behavior outside the home in order to fit into and adapt to the new culture, at home they will act as if they were back in their country of origin.

One-and-a-half-generation individuals are those who immigrated to the United States as young children. Because their contact with the mainstream culture started at an early age, they have been strongly influenced by both their parents' and mainstream cultures; as a result, they are sandwiched between the first and second generations. Their unique experiences can influence their behavior in the work environment. For example, one-and-a-half-generation Latinos may be equally sensitive regarding both Latino and mainstream cultures and may feel equally comfortable in both. Thus, in the work environment, they can help establish bridges between Latino and mainstream colleagues. They represent crucial contacts for companies looking for potential Latino job candidates.

Second-generation Latinos, born in the United States, nevertheless grow up in a home environment that is likely to reflect their parents' country of origin, giving them an opportunity to acquire the values of the Latino culture. Outside the home, the exposure to mainstream culture contributes to their becoming bilingual and bicultural. As children, many act as their parents' interpreters with mainstream Americans. As teenagers, some may lean toward a bilingual, bicultural identity. Others may embrace the mainstream culture and become monolingual English-speakers, but they may still have some knowledge of conversational Spanish and may hold onto some of their parents' cultural values. Third- and fourth-generation Latinos are generally monolingual English-speaking and culturally mainstream. Thus, the fact that an employee has a Spanish surname and is a Latino self-identifier is no guarantee that he or she is bilingual and bicultural.

Intermarriage among subgroups appears to vary by generation. First-generation Latinos tend to marry within their racial and ethnic group. Second- and third-generation Latinos behave differently. As reported recently, 8 percent of immigrant Latinos intermarry, contrasting heavily with 32 percent of second-generation Latinos and 57 percent of those of the third generation and beyond (Edmonston, Lee, and Passel 2002). Some authors have referred to the intermarriage of Latinos from different subgroups as representing the emergence of a Pan-Latino generation (Porter 2001). For example, Mirta, who works as a receptionist, is a Peruvian immigrant married to a second-generation Mexican salesperson. They have made it a point to speak only Spanish to their children at home. On the other hand, Roberto, a sales manager, comments that although his mother is Cuban American and his father is Central American, he does not speak much Spanish.

RELIGION

People from Latin America profess all world religions. It is not unusual to encounter Jewish, Muslim, Protestant, or Buddhist Latinos. An estimated 65 percent, however, are Roman Catholic as a consequence of the Spanish expeditions that initiated the Catholic conversion of indigenous people in 1492 (Warner 2002).

Religion plays a very important role in the lives of many Latinos, and the fact that it is not generally a topic of discussion at work may make some Latinos in the workplace feel isolated. For example, a Cuban American friend of mine (Nilda) noticed this difference during the first year she lived in the United States when coworkers used the expressions "time permitting" or "weather permitting." She preferred to use the expression "God-willing," as was her custom, but she abstained from using this expression at work.

Observance of religious holidays may have an impact in the workplace, as well. Many first-generation Latinos, in particular, may observe Holy Week as if they were in Latin America, where it is celebrated as a weeklong holiday. Their faith may dictate that they participate in church events and rites instead of going to work, reflecting the importance of taking the time to worship rather than making money. As we will discuss further in Chapter 3, Latinos tend to focus on the spiritual rather than the material aspects of life.

RACE

The terms *Latino* and *Hispanic* refer to an ethnicity, not a race. An ethnic group shares common cultural values, history, traditions, and language. Starting in the fifteenth century, English, French, Portuguese, Dutch, and Spanish expeditions visited Latin America, bringing with them African slaves. The physical appearance of Latinos reflects the presence of European colonists as well as combinations of Africans, indigenous Americans, and Asians. Thus, Latinos can be of any race or combination of races; for example, mestizos (European and indigenous), mulattoes (mixed black and European), and zamboes (of mixed indigenous and black ancestry), as well as whites.

Most people from mainland Latin America have some degree of indigenous ancestry. Because the Caribbean islands received a large influx of African slaves, many Spanish-speaking people from these islands use the saying, "*Todos tenemos el negro detrás de la oreja*" ("We all have black behind our ears") to indicate that most likely there was someone of African ancestry in the family.

Closely linked with racial types is the concept of social class in Latin America. In many countries, a small group of families of European Spanish heritage have maintained control of financial empires and dominated land tenancy through political and family alliances. This upper class is generally white and often better educated than other groups. Middle-class Latin Americans represent all races and racial combinations, and many have achieved upward mobility through education. Indigenous groups are generally regarded as belonging to the lower classes in Latin America. Many are underprivileged socially and economically and have had limited access to educational opportunities.

Latinos in the United States exhibit all of the racial combinations that are present in Latin America. Although skin color may reflect a Latino's family origin, it is not indicative of social class or level of income.

EDUCATIONAL ATTAINMENT

Educated Latinos who immigrate to the United States without the initial status of permanent resident are more likely to have access to jobs, higher education, and increased opportunities to legalize their presence in the country than uneducated immigrants, especially if they are undocumented. The latter often perform low-paying, dangerous jobs, with no access to health insurance. This often gives them anonymity and buys them time to legalize their immigration status.

Increasingly, Latinos are attaining higher levels of education. Eleven percent of Latinos 25 years and over reported having completed a bachelor's degree in the 2000 census (Therrien and Ramírez 2001). In the next 10 years, as second- and third-generation individuals continue to find ways to gain access to educational opportunities, they will also have more chances to compete for higher paying jobs. Understanding Latino communication styles will therefore become increasingly essential as employees move from service-sector jobs to supervisory and managerial positions.

CHAPTER THREE

Cultural Values Relevant to the Workplace

Cultural values play a key role in cross-cultural communication. As mentioned earlier, the impact of these values on communication, however, is likely to vary for different generations of Latinos. A supervisor, coworker, or supervisee interested in figuring out how to communicate most effectively with a Latino may first want to find out how many generations the person's family has lived in the United States. For example, a recent (first-generation) immigrant is likely to behave almost exclusively according to his or her own cultural values and may also use Spanish as the primary language. Individuals who are one-and-a-half or second generation are often culturally self-aware and also aware of the norms of the mainstream culture. They are often bilingual and may exhibit behaviors reflecting both cultures. It is useful to keep in mind that some individuals may prefer to switch codes, following mainstream cultural norms at work while maintaining Latino behavior at home. Third- and fourth-generation Latinos generally operate from a mainstream perspective and are often monolingual English speakers. It is wise to avoid categorizing third- and fourth-generation individuals as Latinos solely on the basis of their heritage and name.

Various authors have made significant contributions to the understanding of Latino cultural values. Amado Padilla's pioneering work on Latino acculturation proposes five central Latino cultural values: familism, *simpatía*, *respeto*, gender issues, and time orientation. Other scholars have proposed religiosity, loyalty, and power distance (Marín and Van Oss Marín 1991; Padilla 1980). A managerial perspective suggests another, partially overlapping set of Latino values, including self-worth, dignity and respect, manliness, womanliness, sensitivity, honesty, hierarchy, and religiosity (Kikoski and Kikoski 1999).

On the basis of the literature and of our personal experiences, we suggest eight cultural values that are likely to play a critical role in the workplace: time orientation, *personalismo* (sense of self-worth), simpatía (sensitivity), respeto (respect or dignity), power distance (hierarchy), collectivism, familism, and religion. The sections that follow deal with each of these values in turn. Each section includes a vignette that reflects our personal experiences and illustrates the impact of each of these cultural values in the workplace. Cultural pointers follow each vignette.

TIME ORIENTATION

Many first- and second-generation Latinos are present-oriented and may appear to take a relaxed view of time. For them, being engaged with the present is often more important than thinking about the future. Many Latinos say that the present—what is right in front of them—exists, whereas the future, by contrast, is uncertain. In a way, this is an expression of fatalism, the view that whatever is going to happen is unavoidable regardless of any attempts to intervene and change the order of things. Therefore, they conclude, it is best to take time to smell the roses—to enjoy the present.

From a mainstream perspective, Latinos may appear to be laid-back. Their behavior has led to the Latino "*mañana*" stereotype—the idea that things will get done "tomorrow" in their own time. It is always best, however, to avoid stereotyping and to remember that every person acts differently, on the basis of personal values and priorities. Many Latinos, regardless of generation, are punctual and careful about time because they are focused on performance and on keeping their jobs. And third- and fourth-generation Latinos, like future-oriented mainstream-culture individuals, place a great deal of value on time and often equate it with money.

These contrasting views of time can lead to unwarranted assumptions and biases in the workplace. For example, a mainstream manager may interpret an employee's unexplained tardiness as reflecting a lack of commitment to the organization. On the other hand, when managers, in an attempt to save time, act in a direct, blunt fashion, some Latinos may consider them rude. A cut-to-the-chase, mainstream approach may offend a Latino entrepreneur, who is likely to invest a considerable amount of time trying to get a good sense of a business acquaintance in order to develop the relationship before being open to considering a business deal.

VIGNETTE

ᏯᎧ Andy Allen, a young marketing executive for a tile manufacturing plant in the Midwest, was excited about the prospect of entering the Latin American market. He did not know much about this culture but was sure that the high quality of the tiles his company produced would be enough to make the sale. Because he could not initially travel to Latin America for a face-to-face meeting, Andy decided to mail brochures to prominent construction companies in the region. One of these prospects was Esteban Martínez, a middle-aged Salvadoran engineer specializing in commercial construction, who owned a big company in Central America. After a few days, Andy called to follow up and ensure that his communication had been received.

> *Andy Allen:* Mr. Martínez, this is Andy Allen from the Tile Manufacturing Company in the U.S. I'm calling to confirm that you received our recent promotional brochure.
>
> *Esteban Martínez:* Yes, Mr. Allen, I got your mail.
>
> *Andy:* I hope you've had a chance to look through the materials. Our products are of high quality and are very long-lasting. We want to introduce them to your market.
>
> *Esteban:* Yes, Mr. Allen, I saw them. But it is hard for me to judge this at a distance.

Andy: I understand, Mr. Martínez. I want to assure you that our products are very good. We can also ship promptly. Why don't you try us out? I am confident that you'll be satisfied. I'll even offer you a special introductory price in order to give you a chance to familiarize yourself with our product.

Then Mr. Martínez said something that enlightened Andy in terms of how to deal with Latin Americans:

Esteban Martínez: Mr. Allen, I appreciate your offer very much, but I will not be able to buy from you immediately. First, I need to know you, your company, and your products. I don't know anyone in my market who can give me any reference on you. Knowing people and developing trust takes time. I have built this company based on my timely delivery and the quality of my work. I cannot risk that for a good price from an unknown vendor.

Andy was perplexed, but he began to see things from another perspective. He spoke to his boss and indicated that they probably needed to change their sales strategy for investing in Latin America. Andy's new approach was to invite Mr. Martínez and a group of representatives from four other prominent Latin American construction companies to visit the company headquarters in the U.S., instead of Andy traveling to the Latin American countries with samples of his company's tiles. Such a visit would allow them to introduce themselves and their products to the Latin American prospects.

Andy received his supervisor's approval, and two months later, after careful coordination and multiple conversations, the visit took place. It included several days of meetings with the CEO and the trade specialist, as well as a plant visit to give the potential clients an opportunity to test the quality of the products, examine their top-of-the-line machinery, and see for themselves the care the company took with workers' safety. Andy and Mr. Martínez also had a chance to get to know each other better.

A week after the plant visit, Andy called Mr. Martínez again.

Andy Allen: Mr. Martínez, I hope you enjoyed your visit. What did you think of our products?

Esteban Martínez: Well, Andy, they seem adequate to meet my standards. I am grateful for your courtesies to me. During the past couple of months, I have seen the time you have invested in helping me get to know you and your company. I have become familiar with your financing methods, your people, products, and processes. You have been very responsive to my needs, and so I will place a trial order. Now I feel more confident in trusting your product.

Cultural Pointers

- For Mr. Martínez, getting to know firsthand what he would be buying and the people he would be dealing with required an investment of time in advance of any business negotiations.
- Andy wisely invested time to begin building up a professional relationship, so that Mr. Martínez could develop the sense of comfort he needed before he was ready to buy the tiles.
- For Mr. Martínez, the prestige of his company is linked to his personal name, so he is careful to consider how the quality of new products will affect him.
- The sale required building a relationship and developing trust. Andy was wise enough to work on Mr. Martínez's terms and to give him the information he required to feel confident in making a decision to buy.

PERSONALISMO

One–to–one contact is especially important in the perception of *personalismo,* which pertains to the perceived intrinsic human qualities of individuals who, through their well-meaning interactions, are able to convey warmth and genuine interest in connecting. It is difficult to find an analogy to this cultural value in mainstream behavior because personalismo is based on what Latinos perceive. From a mainstream perspective, personalismo may be described as unbiased, objective, well-intentioned one-to-one interaction exhibited with a personal, caring and respectful attitude.

Latinos respect strangers, peers, and friends who exhibit personalismo. In some cases, even when Latinos have not been introduced to a stranger, they may view the person as having personalismo. For example, a bus driver with whom a Latino may speak once in a while but who shows interest in helping to figure out the best route to get to work may be considered to have personalismo. With respect to peers at work, personalismo refers to perceived aspects of an individual's moral character that lead Latinos to trust him or her. For example, if a Latino has shared experiences with a peer for many years, he or she is likely to believe that double-crossing will not be an issue for concern. A coworker who shares an idea for a better way to carry out a task will be considered to have personalismo, as will a supervisor who acknowledges dedication and recommends employees for annual bonuses. Likewise, a manager who is known for his or her unbiased behavior toward all employees will be seen as having a great deal of personalismo. Such behavior can help develop trust and respect among Latino employees. Perhaps the ultimate test of personalismo occurs when individuals who are united by a long friendship experience a sense that, even setting their friendship aside, they respect and value each other for their intrinsic moral character.

VIGNETTE

෮෮ Sonia Franco is a young Latina working in a collection-processing center in the South. Sonia came to the U.S. to complete her studies and stayed on with this company. She is well educated and efficient, and she has progressed rapidly in her role as a supervisor. She is recognized as being fair with employees and has dramatically increased the productivity of her area. Sonia has a great future ahead of her: she is already being considered for a higher management position in the company.

Although senior management is aware of Sonia's positive attributes, some feel that at times she appears to establish too strong a personal relationship with her direct reports. They believe that this may be an obstacle to Sonia's ability to take on added responsibilities. After some discussion, they decide to ask Francisco, Sonia's longest-serving direct report, to provide input that will help them decide whether her close relationships are making her shortsighted with respect to work decisions. Melissa, the head of human resources, is given the task of talking to Francisco, and he is called in to the HR office.

> *Melissa:* Hello, Francisco. I hope you are doing well. I wanted to talk to you about your supervisor, Sonia. You know we are careful to regularly get our employees' input regarding the performance of their leaders, in order to evaluate opportunities for their professional development. Considering your many years of service, we would like to ask you about your working relationship with Sonia.
>
> *Francisco:* She is a role model to all of us, even to people outside the department, especially the younger employees who are going to school and see that hard work can get you places. I can judge this because I have seen many supervisors come and go during my years at the company.
>
> *Melissa:* That is why we called on you, Francisco. It's good to hear that about Sonia. We like our supervisors to reflect our company values, and it seems you feel she does. How about her decision making with respect to employees?
>
> *Francisco:* We have a great deal of respect for Sonia because she is fair and just. Her decisions are right on track—she always thinks of the company first.
>
> *Melissa:* That's good. But I have heard comments that Sonia gets too involved in the personal lives of the people that work for her.
>
> *Francisco:* Well, if showing that she cares about us as people is getting too involved, then yes. But we value that—it is part of what the

company represents for us. For example, Sonia came to my granddaughter's baptism and my wife's funeral. She often gives me a ride home if I need it. She does not place distance between us. There is no such thing as Sonia being "too involved" or too close to people, especially because she supervises without bias.

Melissa: Do you believe this closeness makes her shortsighted and leads her to make inaccurate decisions about employees?

Francisco: No. In my own case, she questions me when I'm late. She discusses her expectations for my productivity. And I see her doing the same with my peers. She does not let her caring about us get in the way of her responsibilities. I don't think she is shortsighted—I think she has her eyes wide open. In fact, I think we need more people like Sonia in the company. We all trust her. I feel so confident with her that I would follow any instructions she might recommend, even for my personal life. She does the company name proud.

Melissa: Thanks, Francisco. You are always upfront with us.

Cultural Pointers

- Sonia reflects personalismo in the mutual trust that has developed in response to the respect she shows for her employees. Sonia is careful about getting work accomplished, but she does this in a caring way. In return, the employees respect and trust her.

- Latino employees need to perceive that their supervisor cares about them before a sense of trust and respect develops.

- This concept of personalismo is linked to that of simpatía, to be considered next, and this vignette illustrates both traits.

- In tune with her cultural upbringing, Sonia relates to people independently of her position at work.

- Francisco sees Sonia's personal and professional qualities as being blended into the whole individual. He admires and respects her, and it is unlikely that either will attempt to cross the line.

SIMPATÍA

Simpatía is the human quality of engaging in behaviors that promote pleasant social relationships (Marín and Van Oss Marín 1991). Although it is not exactly the same, simpatía resembles the mainstream qualities of being approachable, nice, or charming. But to avoid losing the nuances of the term in an effort to find an equivalent word in English, we will treat simpatía as a distinctly Latino cultural value.

In general, Latinos avoid confrontation and seek harmonious interactions both at home and at work. Within the extended family, aunts and uncles are favorites of children because of their simpatía. Many aunts and uncles become godparents of their brothers' and sisters' children. They proudly and deliberately spoil their nieces and nephews with treats and playful conversations. The relationships grow over time, with aunts and uncles becoming mentors, confidants, and advisers after the children have grown up and become working adults.

In the workplace, simpatía is a key value, one that should not be taken for granted. A supervisor who engages in brief yet pleasant conversations with employees is perceived as simpático or simpática—as having a great deal of simpatía—because of his or her explicit interest in having harmonious relations with employees. On the other hand, a perceived lack of simpatía can be detrimental to the beginning of any relationship with Latino colleagues. A recruiter who even casually expresses confrontational ideas may be perceived as lacking simpatía and may not be able to elicit key information from an interviewee. In order to maintain harmony, and as a sign of respect, the Latino candidate interviewing for a position may carry on until the end of the interview and may appear to agree with the interviewer's perspective. But the Latino has long since written off the interviewer and his or her company. Likewise, lack of simpatía on the part of a supervisor may negatively affect retention of employees, who may become increasingly uncomfortable and eventually decide to seek employment elsewhere.

VIGNETTE

༄ Armando and Manolo, both first-generation Latinos, have worked for the same company for years. Armando, who is the head of marketing, has been going through some rough times at work. He has recently been assigned a new brand of ice cream but has not been achieving the expected results with his marketing campaign. Armando is a peer to Manolo, who is director of operations. They have not always agreed on issues, but they have always looked for opportunities to maintain harmony in their relationship. Now Manolo is concerned about his colleague's performance and his personal well-being. Although he cannot do much to help Armando be more effective, he wants to show his support. Manolo takes the initiative to visit Armando's office more frequently for a cup of coffee and a few minutes of catching up, or to suggest that they have lunch together or even, occasionally, that they go out for drinks at the end of the day.

Armando's mainstream secretary, Brenda, cannot understand the behavior of the two men. She discusses this with Manolo's Latina secretary, Elisa:

> *Brenda:* Elisa, I'm puzzled by Manolo's and Armando's recent behavior, and I thought maybe you could help me understand, since you are a Latina.
>
> *Elisa:* What is it, Brenda? What's troubling you?
>
> *Brenda:* Well, Manolo and Armando have never been close friends. In fact, I know that they've had their disagreements in the past. But as soon as Armando started getting pressure from higher up because the marketing campaign isn't producing the expected results, Manolo has adopted a caring attitude with Armando.
>
> *Elisa:* And what surprises you about that?
>
> *Brenda:* Well, I understand that Armando is going through some difficulties. Business is not good, and so Manolo may want to give

him a shoulder to lean on, but frankly, we each have to deal with our own challenges. This is a professional environment, and I feel there is no room for that kind of thing here. I don't believe Armando asked Manolo for any help.

Elisa: Well, Brenda, this is where their upbringing gives them a common ground. Manolo understands that Armando is going through tough times, and he wants to be there to support him. He perceives that Armando needs a friend to listen to his concerns, and Manolo feels he has an obligation to help him, even if Armando has not asked him to. Armando has accepted this support, which is a license for Manolo to carry it out. I'm sure you are concerned about Armando yourself, but a Latino will be more expressive about feelings and will step in to help. Manolo's concern is real, and his intention is noble.

Cultural Pointers

- Manolo shows caring behavior toward Armando, who appears to need support. Latinos frequently take full ownership of the supportive role.
- Even though he did not expressly ask for help, Armando readily accepts the simpatía and moral support offered by Manolo, with whom he can discuss his work frustration.
- Manolo's attitude toward Armando will most likely mend any flaws in their relationship, because Manolo is there for Armando.
- After the crisis is over and working patterns return to normal, a strong friendship may develop between Armando and Manolo. They will see each other with simpatía, demonstrated through a harmonious and pleasant relationship.
- Should it be required in the future, Armando will do the same for Manolo, because of the vital importance this type of peer support represents among Latinos.

RESPETO

For Latinos, *respeto* (respect) involves the high regard that is granted to a person because of age or position in the hierarchy. Respeto is also a form of admiration, granted—regardless of the individual's social, political, or financial standing—because a person is believed to have intrinsically admirable qualities such as honesty, integrity, or courage. In contrast, in the mainstream culture, respect is often earned, not granted automatically to those in charge.

Age is an important driver for respect. Elderly Latinos often live with the rest of their extended family because the family considers it a duty to care for them. Older generations of Latinos used to teach their children that they should respect their parents—for example, by speaking only when asked to do so by an elder and by following elders' instructions without questioning. Later generations now encourage their children to ask questions, and they value their children's thoughts and ideas; children, in turn, often show appreciation and high regard toward parents who are receptive. Coming from a culture that respects the elderly, many Latinos have a high sense of respect toward peers, supervisors, and managers who are older than they are. They may show this respect by abstaining from expressing contradictory opinions or by trying to help an older colleague to alleviate a heavy workload.

Hierarchical standing also demands respect. This has a direct impact in the work setting. For example, a manager normally enjoys the high regard of Latino subordinates on the basis of his or her position. Acknowledging this attitude can lead to the development of effective working relationships among colleagues or between managers and direct reports. Lack of perceived respect, by contrast, can be detrimental in the workplace. In some instances, the interpretation of respect may be cultural. For example, Latinas appreciate being addressed formally, with title and last name, by male peers. Addressing a Latina by her first name at work should occur only after a working relationship has been established.

At work, Latino employees respect peers who share knowledge unselfishly or who help them avoid potential mistakes. They perceive this sharing of information and willingness to support their work as a sign of integrity and honesty. Latinos also have great respect for colleagues who have the courage to speak up, especially on the group's behalf.

VIGNETTE

☙ Esteban Martínez, a second-generation Latino, has worked for Wayne Fig for five years as head of operations and technology in a web-based game development company. Wayne, who is of mainstream origin, is approaching retirement. He has a number of Latino employees. Esteban has suggested buying new computers for the company in order to increase the capacity to develop more complex web-based games. Aside from the cost of the new computers, this will mean spending money and time on training. Mr. Fig does not agree with Esteban's suggestion because the company's sales have been down. He would prefer not to take the proposal to the board of directors' meeting the following week. Esteban now faces a dilemma based on the respect he has for Mr. Fig: he knows that if the company does not invest in the new computers now, it may continue to lag behind its competitors. On the other hand, he respects Mr. Fig and does not want to go behind his back. He discusses the situation with Omar Suazo, a peer at work.

> *Esteban Martínez:* So, Omar, now you can see my dilemma. I am facing a difficult situation with Mr. Fig's decision, and I don't know what to do.
>
> *Omar Suazo:* Is there any way you can convince Mr. Fig?
>
> *Esteban:* It doesn't seem possible. We have had a number of meetings, and I have also had him speak to a couple of our employees who are familiar with the new equipment. I know that if we don't invest in the new computers now, we could lose market share. This is a high risk for the company to take.
>
> *Omar:* So, why don't you go to another member of the board and explain your case?

Esteban: Well, it's not that simple. Doing something like that would be like contradicting Mr. Fig's decision in public. It would be disrespectful.

Omar: But it's a matter of assessing a risk. Here you are the person with the technical knowledge, and so your opinion should supersede everyone else's.

Esteban: Of course, but Mr. Fig and I have worked together for a long time. However, despite the trust and respect he has for me, in this case he is prioritizing financials over the future. He does not oppose the idea, but he believes the timing is wrong.

Omar: Esteban, I understand your respect for Mr. Fig, but time is of the essence here. If you aren't planning to take extreme measures—like talking to other members of the board—then why are you struggling?

Esteban: Because I have a moral responsibility to the company in my role as technology expert. I feel it's my duty to disclose my concerns and to raise a red flag if I see a risk.

Omar: Well, Esteban, I can't tell you what to do. You'll have to decide for yourself. But tell me—how do you think Mr. Fig will react if you do pursue this idea?

Esteban: Well, he will not be very happy with me, and he will certainly resent my going directly to others.

Omar: So, what are you going to do?

Esteban: Well, Omar, I think I will let Mr. Fig know how I feel and tell him that I am planning to approach several board members to explain my concern and offer my suggestions. He has valid reasons for rejecting the timing of this idea. I trust that the board will evaluate both points of view and take the correct actions.

Omar: Good luck, Esteban. I think that's a good decision. This way, Mr. Fig will be aware of your actions, and you will not feel you are showing a lack of respect for him or going behind his back.

Cultural Pointers

- Esteban verbalizes his respect for Mr. Fig, his supervisor.
- Esteban does not want to contradict Mr. Fig. Doing so would imply questioning the latter's credibility. The natural Latino reaction is to give respect a higher priority than one's professional opinion, especially if trust has developed.
- Esteban faces a dilemma: whether or not to express his professional opinion to others. If he does so, he may come into open conflict with Mr. Fig, his manager, whom he respects. His dilemma is not related to any possible negative consequences that his behavior may have on his professional advancement.

POWER DISTANCE

Power distance may be based on educational, social, or religious standing, as well as on hierarchy at work. This value contrasts significantly with the attitude of the mainstream culture toward those who have high educational, social, or religious standing. In the mainstream culture, individuals may question the behavior of such persons and may interact with them as if they were equals.

Latinos express respect for hierarchy in the form of deferential treatment toward persons they perceive as powerful. For example, some Latinos may see a folk healer or a physician as having an enormous knowledge base regarding health and disease. They will acknowledge the power distance and will show respect by adding titles before the healer's or doctor's first name. Thus, they may address a folk healer as Maestro Elias or the family physician as Doctor Gonzalo.

It is common for Latinos to have high regard for community leaders who, despite huge political or social obstacles, have mobilized the community for the benefit of all. When interacting with such individuals,

Latinos acknowledge the power of these leaders by displaying a great deal of respect.

In the work environment, Latinos treat educated individuals with respect and particularly admire those who have endured sacrifices to complete a college education and who have spent years gaining experience (Warner 2002). Latinos may recognize a manager's experience and knowledge by saying, for example, "Dr. Thomas is right most of the time because she knows what must be done—after all, she has been with the company for more than twenty years."

When power distance is displayed by employees and acknowledged by the manager, a strong sense of mutual respect develops. The employees recognize the manager's place in the hierarchy, and the manager develops a sense of responsibility for the employees' well-being. This can lead to an ideal situation in which the manager or supervisor is not only the formal but also the informal team leader.

Power distance does not always determine the degree of respect a Latino employee gives a supervisor or manager. For example, Latinos may abstain from sharing ideas with a manager whose behavior they dislike. Later, in private, they may say, "I remained silent only because he's the boss, although he doesn't deserve to be in that position."

VIGNETTE

ᏇᎧ Leo Sosa, a second-generation Latino, is the senior trader of an investment company where he manages the trading desk. He has a conversation about salary increases with the firm's human resources director, mainstream-born Diane Johnson, who is at a higher level in the hierarchy than Leo.

> *Leo Sosa:* Diane, now that we are determining employees' salary increases, I wanted to discuss my traders' salaries with you. They have worked hard, and I want to recognize this by compensating them well.

Diane Johnson: That's reasonable, Leo. What are your expectations for salary increases this year?

Leo: A 10 percent increase in their base pay.

Diane: I commend you for thinking of your employees, Leo, but we don't have any justification for granting such a substantial increase. What prompts you to want to do that this year? You know that our financial results have shown deterioration.

Leo: Diane, I agree that it's been a very tough year. The market has been at its lowest in decades. But even so, my traders put forth their best effort to get business and they've had positive results. I want to compensate them for this. The company needs to show its appreciation for their hard work in both good and bad times.

Diane: I understand, Leo. However, the market study we conducted through a well-recognized consulting firm shows that similar companies are only minimally increasing salaries—3 percent, tops, for traders. Before the current financial crisis started, your people were already the best-paid traders in this market. You need to take that into account. I just don't see how we can justify a 10 percent increase.

Leo: I know, Diane, but I'm afraid we'll lose our best traders if they don't see a future here. Other firms will lure them with higher entry salaries. This is my way of protecting and retaining them. Hopefully, compensating them well will also make your life easier in terms of not having to hire new traders.

Diane: True. That would help. However, you know that human resources is my specialty. I take good care to consult with external experts and also to consider market trends. Your proposal is simply unreasonable.

Leo: I see your point of view, Diane, but I don't know how else I can hold on to them. How about a 7 percent increase, then?

Diane: We're moving in the right direction, Leo, but I don't think we can grant more than 3 percent. Why don't we revisit the situation in six months to see if any adjustments are needed? Meanwhile, I will work with you to keep the traders motivated.

Leo: You know I'm not happy with that, Diane, but let's do it. You're the expert. I have to trust what you tell me because I know you have the knowledge and you've always been right in the past. I'll convey the message to my employees.

Diane: And I will work with you, Leo, to identify other nonmonetary incentives to help us retain them. Please keep me posted on how it goes.

Cultural Pointers

- Leo feels he needs to protect his employees. He wants to compensate them for their efforts—not only for their results.
- Diane is the subject-matter expert, so she comes back with a series of facts. Power distance is established by Diane's greater knowledge of the subject, which finally leaves Leo without an argument.
- The facts are irrefutable; Leo respects Diana's knowledge. He accepts her rationale and modifies his initial proposal.

COLLECTIVISM

In the mainstream culture, self-reliance is considered a virtue, and every person is expected to operate individually and to take responsibility for his or her own destiny. Thus, individualism and independence are highly valued and are ingrained in children from an early age (Althen 2003; Stewart and Bennett 1991; Wanning 2003).

By contrast, Latino behavior is permeated by collectivism, exhibited as interdependence for the sake of harmonious relations with peer groups or family members. Existence is viewed from a group perspective rather than from the individualistic perspective of the mainstream. Latinos also prefer to be in the company of others because social interactions provide personal satisfaction and self-assurance. The shared values of the social or work group strengthen the group and provide a sense of belonging for

Latinos. It has been reported that even Latino executives rank high in collectivism (Hofstede 1980; Kikoski and Kikoski 1999).

Latinos often go to great lengths to show that they are sensitive to the concerns of the entire group, and they often express a sense of collective responsibility for facing and resolving both group and individual problems. In the workplace, one common situation occurs when employees who are dissatisfied with specific aspects of the work environment meet in informal settings outside work to discuss their shared problems. An informal leader often emerges, and it is understood that the most important aspect of the discussion is to resolve the problems that the group has encountered for the benefit of all.

Collectivism may be used in a manner similar to the way the mainstream culture's concept of *teamwork* is applied in the workplace. The sense of a collective spirit can be an effective tool for motivating Latino employees and for promoting productivity because they are generally very open to ideas that will benefit the majority of employees.

VIGNETTE

༺༻ Jaime Mella emigrated from Latin America to the United States 30 years ago, looking for a better quality of life and more job opportunities. He built a small but solid landscaping business that now has 50 employees, including many immigrants, in jobs ranging from administrative to gardening tasks.

Jaime's son Jimmy, born and raised in the U.S., recently completed a business degree. He has many ideas for improving the family business, and here he presents some of them to his father.

> *Jimmy Mella:* Dad, one of the areas we need to change is the company's hiring policies. You have always hired recent immigrants. Granted, they're hard-working, but some don't have very good language skills. Maybe we should look for a different profile when we hire.

Jaime Mella: That is an interesting idea, son, but how would that improve our service? Why should we change?

Jimmy: Well, if we hire trained, English-proficient workers, the quality of our service and our relationship with clients would improve.

Jaime: Son, I'm really proud to see all you have learned, but real life is not like books. When I arrived in this country, I found people who helped me even though I did not speak the language and did not have a lot of schooling. They trusted me and gave me a decent job. I succeeded and was able to build my own company after some time. I trust the people we hire will work equally hard and progress as well.

Jimmy: I know that, Dad, and I know you are very grateful to those who gave you an opportunity, but we're talking about different times here. Our business demands more highly skilled workers if we're going to stay ahead of our competitors.

Jaime: I see your point of view, but I'm not sure I want to sacrifice giving others an opportunity similar to what I had when I came here, even if it means losing some business. After all, this has been the profile I have always used, and look at the company I have been able to build. This is the way I will give back to society what I have received. It's the philosophy that has guided my work and life.

Jimmy: Dad, I understand now. Why don't we work through this some other way? What if I design a new program to give the employees basic training on the machinery we use? We know that sometimes the equipment breaks down because they don't know how to use it.

Jaime: I like what I hear, son! This will allow our current employees to become more proficient with the equipment. Could we also include some basic conversational English classes? I want to help them adjust to this society.

Jimmy: I think it's doable. It won't cost us a lot, and we will be helping our employees.

Jaime: Son, you make me proud. I feel confident I will leave this company in good hands in the future.

Cultural Pointers

- Belonging to and giving back to the community are of high importance for Jaime, reflecting his sense of collectivism.
- Jaime is willing to sacrifice revenue and volume of work on behalf of the people working for him.
- Jaime places more importance on giving someone an opportunity than on getting a highly trained employee.
- Jimmy understands and respects his father, but because of his professional background, he places a higher priority on business success and productivity.
- Jimmy also shows collectivism by finding a way to support his father's thinking of the collective and wishing to protect his Latino employees in a way that does not completely rule out Jimmy's original objective of upgrading the profile of the workers.
- Jimmy shows his understanding and reflects some collectivism in maintaining harmonious relationships with his father, despite their difference in priorities. To safeguard the relationship, Jimmy finds a way to accomplish his goal of creating a more highly skilled workforce through a method that makes Jaime feel he has not lost what he considers his highest priority: his collective concern for helping others.

FAMILISM

Familism, the sense of the importance of family, may appear to be a subset of collectivism. It is one of the most important Latino cultural values. The Latino family includes members of both the nuclear and the extended family, who are often closely tied together by sentiments of respect, loyalty, and unity. All members must abide by these principles without questioning them.

The Latino family is a matriarchal organization. Although the father is the authority figure, he often spends most of his time outside the house working to fulfill his duties as a provider, while the mother takes care of the house and the children. As women carry out their maternal duties in the United States, they gradually manage to acquire a great deal of power because their responsibilities demand that they get out of the house more often than they would in their own culture. For example, when Latinas fill out forms in public offices, take their children to school, buy groceries at the produce market, and go to church, they meet other women, share information, learn about existing resources, and make decisions. Consequently, they become actively involved in community life and develop strong social support networks.

Family ranks as the number one concern for Latino workers (Kleiman 2002; Sabogal, Marín, and Otero-Sabogal 1987). When family members get together on weekends, they eat and drink together and the group sharing experience serves as an outlet for confiding work-related fears, concerns, plans, and dreams to all family members. It provides an opportunity, sometimes, to make fun of their tribulations at work and to seek advice from family members who have more experience.

For Latinos, having a job is important first and foremost because it is the source of income that helps support the family. Even in the workplace, family remains the number one priority. Therefore, factors that may affect the family may be strong motivators to encourage higher employee productivity. For example, for some Latinos, having time off to spend with the family may be as important as getting a raise in pay is for mainstream individuals. For many Latinos, "time off" means significant periods of time to go on trips with family members, not just time off to care for children. Besides, day care is not a serious issue for many Latinos because grandmothers, aunts, or cousins are generally readily available to care for children. For other Latinos, higher compensation may be as critical as it is for members of the mainstream culture because it may represent the possibility of buying a house for the family. Therefore, it is important to be familiar with the priorities of individual Latino employees when recruiting new hires or when considering offering a promotion.

VIGNETTE

૭ᴠᴏ María Rodríguez, a first-generation Latina immigrant, has worked in the accounting department of an Internet sales company for only a few months. Her father, who had been ill once before, recently fell ill again. With a sick parent at home, Maria, a single mother of two, struggles to go to work every day. Her lack of rest and multiple worries has a negative impact on her performance. Tammy Hendrick, her supervisor, calls her into her office and puts her on notice: if her performance does not improve, she could be fired.

As she sat on the train on her way home, María talked the situation over with Nieves Allende, her longtime Latina friend, reflecting on a past experience.

> *María Rodríguez:* Nieves, my supervisor, Miss Hendrick, called me in today to discuss my performance. First she said some nice things about my work the first few months after I joined the company, but then she said that my performance had changed.
>
> *Nieves Allende:* I'm sad to hear that, María. But I'm guessing there may be some truth there, considering all your worries with your dad and the children.
>
> *María:* You're right. I know I'm not the same. But how can I focus on productivity with everything I have going on at home? I accept that my work has deteriorated, but that's not what worries me.
>
> *Nieves:* No? Then what is on your mind?
>
> *María:* I'm upset about her insensitivity. She indicated I needed to go the human resources department to discuss my situation and consider taking a leave of absence. Not once did she ask about my dad or offer her personal support.
>
> *Nieves:* Well, María, actually she did everything according to how these issues are supposed to be handled in the U.S. She stated the facts and gave you the professional solution to your problem.

María: Sure, Nieves, but that's not what I expected. I really miss my previous supervisor, Mr. José Santana, at the company I worked for last year.

Nieves: How was his behavior different from Miss Hendrick's?

María: Well, when my dad got sick last year, he reacted very differently. When he heard Dad had been hospitalized, Mr. Santana and his wife visited to let me know they cared. I discussed my pending work openly with him and was able to work from home when my dad required my presence. He helped me so I did not fall behind in my work. His sense of caring, his support, his understanding of the difficult situation I was going through—that really helped.

Nieves: He sounds like a very caring person.

María: He was. He continuously asked how I was holding up, what he and the company could do to help. And they did help, in things such as child care, in-home medical support, and loans for medical expenses. Mr. Santana was like family.

Nieves: It's great to have people like that in your life, María. But I don't think Miss Hendrick was really singling you out in any way. She was just following company policy.

María: Well, if I have to lose my job because I need to take care of my father and my children, so be it. After all, that is more important than anything in the world to me. I'm the head of the household and I need to provide, but I also need to take care of my family in other ways. They are all I have in life.

Nieves: Yes, María, I agree. There are many jobs out there, but there is only one family. They need you now, so you must find a way to deal with the situation.

María: You're right, Nieves. I'll go to the human resources department tomorrow to see what I can arrange. But if nothing works out, I'm sorry to have to say, I will need to put my family's needs first, whatever the implications will be. God will provide!

Cultural Pointers

- ↞ María compares her two supervisors, indicating a preference for Mr. Santana, the Latino supervisor, who included familism in his relationship with her. She expected to find support, a caring attitude, protection, and understanding from her current supervisor, Miss Hendrick, and is upset by her attitude.
- ↞ This is in tune with her priority of family ahead of work, pay, and professional development. She sees her responsibility in caring for loved ones as more important than bringing in the money to fulfill their needs.
- ↞ María is willing to lose her job if it gets in the way of fulfilling her responsibilities as mother and daughter.

RELIGION

For many Latinos, religion has a strong impact on social life and daily activities. They feel a profound reverence toward God and other powerful divine forces, such as the Virgin Mary and various saints and angels. These divine beings are often invoked and asked to intercede with God to provide help for a family member or assistance in resolving a problem at work.

Religion affects behavior at work because many Latinos consider God as the giver of everything: health, work, and family (Alcalay, Sabogal, and Gribble 1992). In addition, for some, religious faith is linked with a fatalistic view of life, an acceptance of the inevitable. Thus, the state of a person's health or work life may be deemed a consequence of God's approval or disapproval of that person's behavior. Thus, many Latinos observe religious celebrations with fervor in order to remain in good standing with God.

In the United States, Latino behavior regarding religious issues may vary as a consequence of the degree of adjustment to mainstream culture, geographical distance to churches, the existence or lack of a support network, or generational differences. New immigrants and first-generation Latinos may be more attached to religious rituals and may observe religious holidays with more dedication than second-, third-, and fourth-generation mainstream Latinos.

In some Latin American countries, doing business on religious holidays can be seen as inappropriate. Religious holidays are generally observed as national holidays in most Latin American countries. Therefore, attempting to hold meetings on one of these holidays is out of the question. This contrasts with the mainstream culture's attitude toward religion, where personal feelings regarding religion and faith are not likely to be shared in the workplace.

VIGNETTE

౬౨ Tom Hughes, of mainstream origin, is the sales manager for an agricultural equipment company. He has been successful with some Latin American businesses and has made it a goal to visit his clients personally twice a year. This time, Tom flew to South America with the goal of increasing his sales volume. He felt he had already built a relationship with his clients and figured he could close some deals by the end of the week. He knew from previous trips that business in Latin America was relaxed and informal, so he figured that, once there, he would be able to focus on making the necessary appointments and meeting key people. He had done so on previous occasions, and his clients had always welcomed him and made time for him.

As soon as he arrived, Tom called several of his clients. To his surprise, he found that none of them were available: "Tom, it's Holy Week," each one said in turn. "We can't see you until next week."

Frustrated, Tom decided to stay until the holidays were over and then meet with his clients. As he was sitting by the hotel's bar, he met Alberto Sánchez, a travel agent who worked in New York and was visiting his family. Tom explained his ordeal.

Tom Hughes: Mr. Sánchez, I'm in total shock! I don't see how the whole country can close up for an entire week for a religious holiday.

Alberto Sánchez: I can understand your frustration, because in the U.S. we work on most religious holidays. But religion is a huge part of people's lives here, and companies recognize this. For us, this holiday is somewhat like your Thanksgiving. It's a time to be with family.

Tom: Sure, and I can respect that—but I'm still surprised that they couldn't make some time for me. After all, business is business, and I traveled quite a distance to see them.

Alberto: It just doesn't work that way, Mr. Hughes. In Latin America, religious events are sacred. Business simply does not take priority over religious practices, and they don't happen at the same time. In order to do business successfully in Latin America, you'll probably need to be more sensitive to what's important to people here.

Tom: In any case, I'm planning to let them know how I feel. After all, I've had to pay for extra days at the hotel. Basically, I've been forced to take a vacation here, because I traveled all this way and then was unable to meet with anyone.

Alberto: Well, you can do that if you wish, but your clients probably already think you are very insensitive to even suggest meeting with them on these dates, and if you now press your case, they will feel even more resentful.

Tom: Really? I guess I see your point.

Alberto: I suggest you apologize to them once you meet. If you don't, you may lose some of the camaraderie and trust you have developed, and you'll jeopardize your opportunities for additional business and relationships. Then this trip would really be a total failure for you. Next time, plan your trip more carefully.

Tom: Mr. Sánchez, I can't say I understand or feel comfortable with the situation, but I do appreciate your helping me see the importance of religious traditions for my clients here. I'll certainly consider your suggestions.

Cultural Pointers

- Most Latin Americans have great respect for religion. Even if they do not regularly practice rituals, they acknowledge religious holidays.
- Tom's clients, true to their culture, place higher priority on religion than on business.
- The clients use the religious holidays to share time with family and to reflect on the meaning of the event. They do not even consider meeting Tom, which would interfere with the religiosity of the events.
- Tom's insensitivity, especially if he verbalizes it, may harm the relationship he has been able to build with his Latin American clients. Alberto senses this and becomes more straightforward with Tom. In fact, he is somewhat upset by Tom's lack of sensitivity.
- Latin Americans live in close-knit communities linked by relationships, so if Tom discloses his true sentiments to any of his clients, this may affect his dealings with other potential clients, as well.
- When doing business with individuals of another culture, it is always important to become familiar with their customs and traditions and to demonstrate a tolerance for and understanding of their beliefs.

Communication Styles of Latinos

Joe McNulty, vice president for customer service at the UTT Telephone Company, asks his two star employees, Carlos López, manager for the Spanish-speaking team and their customers, and Frank Rose, manager for the English-speaking team and their customers, to instruct all of their customer service representatives to decrease by 10 percent the average time they spend speaking with customers on the phone. "We need to optimize our efficiency by handling more calls," he explains. When Joe asks Carlos and Frank if they have any questions, Frank asks about the timeline Joe has in mind to accomplish the goal, while Carlos comments that it may take his representatives some time to adjust to the new directive. So confident is Joe in the skills that Frank and Carlos have that he proposes that they consider the implementation process as a competition between the two teams. Frank dashes out of Joe's office, making a mental list of possible strategies he can use to win. Carlos, on the other hand, calls his mentor to discuss his problem: he's not sure he understands what his boss really wants. He believes that Joe may be asking for the impossible, which will set him up for failure and force him to leave the company. In his view, shortening the length of conversations with Spanish-speaking customers is an unreasonable and counterproductive goal.

What went wrong? Joe McNulty gave direct instructions and, when neither of his managers pushed back, assumed that there was agreement. In reality, Frank was in agreement, but Carlos was not. Carlos did not ask direct questions out of respect for his boss and also because he did not want to do so in front of a colleague who seemed to understand the directions and appeared to agree with the goal. Carlos chose to appear agreeable to maintain harmony. He took an indirect approach to expressing his concern, sharing only that his team would need time to implement Joe's idea. Had Joe asked for opinions instead of questions, Carlos would have explained that Latinos need more time on the phone, that Joe's idea was not culturally appropriate, and that it was unlikely to work for his team.

The situation described here will probably have a negative impact on the organization. When difficult situations arise in cross-cultural communication, expectations may not be met and miscommunication may result. In such cases, comprehending Latinos' various communication styles is key to success in the work environment. Effective communication is crucial when it comes to giving directions, discussing performance issues, explaining promotions, and dealing with other personnel actions.

Although communication styles may vary from one person to another, there are basic cultural issues that characterize many verbal and nonverbal interactions with Latinos. The impact of such cultural values appears to be significant for employees at all levels. Even Latino executives often rank high in collectivist or group-oriented communication styles, showing respect and sensitivity in their interpersonal relationships.

Feelings and emotions have a strong impact on Latinos' thought processes, and they are often incorporated into conversations, decisions, and the perspective of a discussion. For example, some Latinos may share a rich description of the professional, emotional, and family-related factors that led to a work-related decision, even before announcing the actual decision.

When René Rodriguez, a shift manager at a fast-food restaurant, convenes his staff to announce a promotion, he begins with a story that describes his young son's school achievements and how this led him to believe that it was time to promote a member of his staff. Only after telling the story does he reveal the name of the recipient of the promotion. Most likely the mainstream employees were very confused by this storytelling and wondered what the son's achievement had to do with the promotion. By contrast, the Latino employees trusted that René was going somewhere with his approach and waited for him to get there. They understood that someone who did well in school would probably work well and get promoted. This approach contrasts with many workplace discussions that take place among mainstream individuals. Unlike Latinos, they are likely to announce a decision and then describe the decision-making process succinctly, in a rational way, placing emphasis on the business case. Their focus is to support the decision with evidence.

Understanding differences in communication styles between the Latino and the mainstream cultures is one of the keys to developing harmonious relations in the workplace. The following sections will focus on Latino verbal and nonverbal communication styles.

VERBAL COMMUNICATION

Knowing an employee's country of origin can provide useful information for understanding the logic behind the flow of conversations and ideas.

Flow of Conversation Taking turns is expected in workplace discussions, but this may present a challenge when people from different Latin American countries meet to discuss business. In general, those who can capture the attention of a group have a greater chance to use their turn and to keep it for as long as they have something to say. Without attempting to stereotype, a number of widely accepted country-specific behaviors reinforce this point. Mexicans, Argentinians, and Chileans are generally talkative and often seek to capture the attention of the group at the beginning of a meeting. Mexicans are known for expressing pride in the ways of their country of origin when they discuss almost any subject. They have a saying, "*Lo hecho en México, está bien hecho*" ("What is made in Mexico is well made"). It is not uncommon to hear them say "*Viva México!*" as a closing statement at informal gatherings. Argentinians tend to be loquacious and engage in long discussions into which they may weave unrelated topics such as their country's politics, economy, and soccer team. A common joke among Latin American professionals is that all others must attempt to share their message before Argentinians take their turn because they may exhaust the time allotted for everyone. This is not seen as rude but rather as a national trait. Chileans, by contrast, wait for their turn, use a reasonable amount of time, and often engage in highly intellectual discussions. Brazilians have no problem interrupting a discussion, and they tend to speak their minds very freely and at a fast pace. People from Central America generally study their listeners carefully and then share their message in a timely fashion when their turn comes. Most want to be courteous and cautious, and they tend to take special care to say only what is appropriate and expected.

Flow of Ideas Before making their main statement, most Latinos will offer a great deal of information that is intended to help set the stage and prepare the listener for the message. This lengthy preparation may seem odd to mainstream individuals given that, in their culture, the main idea or message is stated first, followed by the supporting information or rationale. Why do Latinos speak in this way? One reason may be the desire to connect and seek harmony before disclosing information that they believe their listeners may not find agreeable. By seeking harmony, they are also showing a respectful attitude. What mainstream individuals may perceive as a pointless preamble is actually as important as the message itself and should receive close attention. In working with Latinos, it is always wise to look for the message beyond the words. Very often, Latino politicians exhibit this behavior when they address their communities by engaging in vivid recollections of their families' struggles as immigrants. Only after discussing many details do they share their political views and ask for the audience's votes.

DIRECT VERSUS INDIRECT APPROACH

Mainstream individuals are often direct when asked to state their views or to respond to questions. By contrast, Latinos may or may not use a direct approach, depending on the issues at stake. In cases in which cultural values may be affected, they often use an indirect style to communicate.

Direct Approach   For Latinos, a direct approach is preferred only when the message does not threaten harmonious relations by having the potential to create dissent. Latinos find agreement easier to handle than disagreement. Unlike mainstream individuals, Latinos tend to play it safe: they simply avoid asking direct questions or making direct statements. This behavior may be disconcerting to a non-Latino manager or supervisor, but it should in no way be interpreted as signifying a lack of motivation or a shortage of opinions. In fact, it is simply an indication of respect for hierarchy, a value that is ingrained in Latinos from childhood (see the discussion of "power distance" in Chapter 3). Children are told, "*Los niños no opinan en las conversaciones de adultos*" ("Children don't make comments in adult conversations"), and they learn to hold back their thoughts until they are given permission to speak. Thus, not volunteering a conflicting opinion may be a way of showing respect for the person who represents authority and may be an acknowledgment of being in a subordinate position from an administrative perspective.

If encouraged to share an opinion, however, even low-income and partially educated Latino employees may readily offer their point of view. A manager who asks Latino staff members to propose a meeting date may be offered several dates, along with the comment that everyone's schedule is flexible. But if, instead of asking for a date, the manager asks for opinions regarding different proposed dates, staff members will likely share them.

Asking direct questions related to the job is often a challenge for Latinos because, in their view, doing so may indicate that they lack the necessary skills to perform the job or to understand instructions. Thus, asking Latinos direct questions such as "What does the manual say about this?" or "What are the criteria for selection of vendors?" may produce anxiety; they may fear losing their job or looking bad in front of others. For many Latino employees, maintaining harmony with the boss is crucial because it can help protect the family from having to endure the financial hardships that could result if they are fired.

Indirect Approach Most Latinos prefer to use an indirect approach when communicating with a supervisor because this increases their sense of comfort and safety. Thus, they may refer to their own personal issues as if they were other people's issues. While waiting for an opportunity to speak indirectly, Latinos may appear to adopt a passive stance as they wait for a chance to speak up. This attitude should not be interpreted as a sign of passivity; it is only a cultural approach that helps to maintain harmony and avoid confrontation. Although this indirect approach to communication may require more time, it is, nevertheless, a clear effort to communicate thoughts. It should not be interpreted as a strategy to withhold information or as an attempt to be dishonest.

Sometimes a Latino employee may contribute to the discussion using the third person (*he, she, they*) instead of the first person (*I, we*). For example, the employee may describe a situation from the perspective of an observer. In this way, the speaker develops a comfort zone within which to vent thoughts that would not otherwise be communicated. Thus, an employee who is dissatisfied with the work schedule may suggest that "some company employees" are having a hard time arriving at work promptly because their start time coincides with rush hour on the freeway. This approach may also be used to discuss inappropriate behavior of supervisors, unhappiness regarding low compensation, the absence of benefits, and other issues.

Another indirect style of communication occurs when employees speak for the group in order to bring up an issue that has personal impact. For example, an employee may say, "Holy Week is coming up. Some people may want to take time off." When Latino employees take this indirect approach, they are reflecting a collectivist attitude, not a desire to assume a leadership role for the given group. The employee may be defending a point that will help establish harmony among workmates while also resolving a personal matter.

Even when there is an urgent need to set the record straight regarding performance issues, Latinos may opt to use an indirect approach. For example, they may state that other employees have been performing a certain task in the same manner as the speaker.

Rituals, Self-Disclosure, Disagreements, and Arguments If there is one ritual that most Latinos share, it is the use of humor to establish a relationship. Telling a joke is a way of showing openness with someone with whom the speaker feels comfortable. When two people share jokes, it means that the formal relationship is moving toward a more relaxed one and that barriers are coming down. Once this transition has been made, the door is open to doing business; this is the beginning of a close business relationship. It is appropriate to acknowledge this openness appreciatively by saying, "That was a great joke—I hope I can remember it to share it with my friends."

Self-disclosure is very special for Latinos. Many enjoy sharing personal stories to pave the way toward doing business. They spontaneously share both their own and others' experiences. Telling a personal story to a potential business acquaintance or colleague at work is a way of saying, "I'm sharing this with you because I trust you and I'd like to get to know you better. Can you tell me more about yourself?" Although some mainstream-culture individuals may see this as a waste of time, it is important to take the cue: if the sharing is not reciprocated, it may not happen again for a long time.

In general, and especially in the work environment, Latinos avoid disagreements and arguments at almost all costs. Their preference is to avoid sharing their thoughts even if their apparently nonconfrontational attitude may be perceived as passive. Some individuals may think that things are unlikely to change even if they speak up, and this strong belief may discourage them from trying to clarify issues with a supervisor by sharing their point of view. They may believe that, regardless of the attempt, the situation is bound to remain unchanged. Thus, although a supervisor may intend to initiate an exchange of thoughts and opinions, the employee may choose not to verbalize opinions or may become covertly defensive. This choice is made in the belief that it is best to carry out orders or tasks they disagree with and simply survive difficult times to the degree possible rather than engage in a confrontational discussion. In addition to being a fatalistic attitude, this behavior is also an example of familism: after the family itself, employment has a high priority because it is equated with the employee's—and therefore the family's—survival (Kikoski and Kikoski 1999).

There is one situation in which a Latino employee may engage in a direct confrontation. A strong disagreement involving disrespect toward a female family member or for the employee's honorable reputation may trigger an emotional reaction that in turn may lead to passionate verbal conflict.

Formal/Informal Behavior In the business environment, Latinos tend to be very formal. They often greet a new acquaintance with a nod and a handshake. In subsequent meetings, the level of formality may decrease and they may place a hand on the other person's arm or shoulder while they offer a handshake. This may evolve over the years to a brisk hug (*abrazo*) among men or a brief kiss on the cheek between men and women or between two women.

This transition from formal to informal behavior tends to occur regardless of whether the other person is a superior or a subordinate. A mainstream manager should interpret this shift as positive, because Latinos will not make this transition to more informal behavior unless they are at ease. A mainstream subordinate should appreciate this openness because, in the current environment, Latino managers tend to be extremely reserved as they become upwardly mobile in the belief that mainstream behavior is an asset in a highly competitive professional environment. That said, in some Latin American countries, this level of formality is often waived. Such would be the case for an interviewee referred by someone the interviewer knows very well, which automatically establishes a link between them. It may also include the case of a business acquaintance visiting a person along with someone who is already close to that person.

NONVERBAL COMMUNICATION

Nonverbal communication includes forms of communication other than spoken words that contribute to delivering a message. It can involve interpersonal distance, silence, gestures, touch, eye contact, and facial expressions. Understanding how these factors operate in the work setting can be helpful in establishing effective, culturally appropriate communication with Latinos.

Interpersonal Distance On average, personal space is about 14 or 15 inches for Latinos. This contrasts sharply with European Americans' preferred distance of between 18 inches and four feet.

In the business environment, formal distance for Latinos is about the distance between two individuals seated in front of and behind a desk, respectively. Distance in a casual work relationship is often 14 to 15 inches. Distance in intimate relationships is closer than 14 inches.

At times, some Latinos may inadvertently decrease their interpersonal distance from mainstream individuals to the point of creating discomfort. A mainstream person who is not familiar with Latino culture may consider the distance intrusive or misinterpret the behavior as a desire to establish personal intimacy. A male Latino business acquaintance recently shared with us that years after he retired, he found out that his mainstream male boss had always believed that our Latino acquaintance was trying to make a pass at him because of the degree of physical closeness he had maintained while they were discussing business matters at work. When in doubt about how to handle an uncomfortable distance situation, it is best to stand up as if you are looking for a document or to move away in a natural manner; stepping back or moving away abruptly may be considered offensive. Again, it is useful to remember that variations exist among Latinos. For example, South Americans tend to be more distant physically than Central Americans, with Mexicans somewhere in the middle.

Role of Silence Although most mainstream individuals are accustomed to communicating their thoughts openly when they feel they must clarify situations in the workplace, many Latinos, as we've said earlier, prefer to abstain from sharing ideas or concerns with authority figures or with those who, in their view, may not be sensitive to them. In this instance, Latinos may be more comfortable remaining silent.

When silence is an issue for a mainstream manager or colleague, the best approach is to ask Latinos to share their opinion. Doing this opens the door to dialogue, because sharing is very important for Latinos; it is part of their collectivist value system. Moreover, expressing an opinion is seen as voicing a personal view, not as stating a firm attitude or commitment. By the same token, when Latinos notice that a manager or peer remains silent, they may become increasingly concerned because they may see this silence as a sign of lack of agreement or harmony.

Arrangement of Furniture Most Latinos are very sociable and enjoy engaging in conversations that may start as a business meeting and end as the beginning of a friendship. At work, they often place their chairs close together. If available, they may prefer to sit on a sofa, because this creates a more relaxed environment for talking and sharing.

Latinos often prominently display photographs of dear ones as a way of expressing pride in the family. It is appropriate for colleagues to comment on these pictures: "Are these your children? What a handsome family!" or "I see that you have teenagers. That is a difficult age for parents." A few minutes will often be spent on a conversation on this topic. This contrasts with the mainstream culture's custom of hanging diplomas and certificates and displaying awards to provide visitors with visible highlights of a successful professional career.

Gestures Many Latinos take pride in saying that they "talk with their hands." They often move their hands to highlight aspects of the conversation. At times, they may also raise their arms to capture attention while they are describing or discussing specific aspects of a project. These gestures are performed simultaneously and automatically in conversation, as if they were another element of spoken language.

When the level of emotion is high, Latinos may turn their heads as if to whisper and may simultaneously reach out and touch their listener's arm as they speak, while diminishing the distance between themselves and the other person.

If engaging in very emotional discussions or presentations, some Latinos may hit the table or the podium with an open hand to emphasize a point; Latino politicians do this very frequently.

Touch Latinos are a contact culture. That is, they often expect and make physical contact. As in the mainstream culture, encounters with business acquaintances often begin and end with a handshake between men and between men and women. With closer acquaintances at the same administrative level, some Latinos may shake hands while briefly patting the other individual on the shoulder. It is also acceptable for a supervisor to do this with a good employee as a sign of approval. However, a subordinate should not pat the shoulder of a supervisor unless they have developed a close working relationship, generally over a period of several years. Kisses and embraces are generally reserved for family members, close friends, and well-known business acquaintances. Among many Latinos, the use of touch is somewhat more relaxed and acceptable among new acquaintances when used as a way of establishing immediate empathy. This is generally reserved for interaction between Latinos, however, as they know better than to engage in such informal behavior the first time they meet a mainstream person.

Eye Contact Latinos engage in eye contact that is more intense and prolonged than that exhibited by European American, African American, and Asian American immigrants (Ting-Toomey 1999). In business settings in general, eye contact should be brief and intermittent. Latinos believe that making eye contact is a sign of sincerity that signals good intentions. Thus, during a conversation, eye contact can help establish a level of trust between manager and employee, regardless of which one is Latino. The speaker often actively seeks eye contact first, while the listener acknowledges the intent by meeting the speaker's eyes.

If, however, either manager or employee is a woman, eye contact should *not* be an intense gaze. Instead, it should be brief and repeated several times during the conversation, and the attitude should stay at a formal level to convey respect. Avoiding sustained eye contact can be a sign of respect and an acknowledgment of authority when a subordinate is conversing with a supervisor.

Facial Expressions Latinos are very expressive people, often using intense facial expressions to accentuate or highlight comments. Raising the eyebrows, frowning, smiling, or a combination of these may express satisfaction, conviction, surprise, or frustration. Latinos are also very sensitive to the facial expressions of others, especially those of the mainstream culture, given their inherent desire to please, be accepted, and gain approval.

The following vignette contrasts mainstream and Latino cultural communication styles.

VIGNETTE

෩ Antonio González is a branch manager who supervises 10 employees at a bank. A one-and-a-half-generation Latino, he emigrated with his parents from El Salvador when he was 5. Antonio has a bachelor's degree and is bilingual and bicultural. He understands the cultural issues of both the mainstream culture and his parents' culture and deliberately uses this knowledge to deal with situations that arise with all those who report to him.

Two weeks earlier, Antonio had sent a memo to all his direct reports asking for volunteers to work overtime in order to meet the bank's goals. He had hoped that all his supervisees would sign up, but that was not the case. Now he is meeting individually with Michael and José, the only two of his reports who did not volunteer to work overtime. Pay close attention to the difference in approaches he uses with these two employees.

> *Antonio González:* Thank you for your willingness to see me before your shift starts. I've been meaning to meet with you for about a week. (*He offers a brief handshake.*)

Michael: Sure. No problem.

Antonio: Michael, I want to inform you that we're close to missing our target goals for this year. One of the strategies that we've implemented is to offer extended hours at this branch to attract more clients. You've probably seen the ads on television.

Michael: Yes, I've seen them.

Antonio: I'd like to know whether you're going to be able to work overtime during the coming months, so I can plan ahead.

Michael: I've had some personal issues lately, but I can make arrangements. I just didn't know it was that serious.

Antonio: Yes, it is. That's why I need your support. It's great to know you'll be able to help! I knew I could count on you! (*He offers a handshake.*)

Two hours later Antonio meets with José. He notices that José is tense and worried.

Antonio: Hi, José. How's the family? (*He makes eye contact with José and shakes his hand, then sits on the sofa, beside him.*)

José: The family is growing. My wife's pregnant again. We're having our second baby in three more months.

Antonio: Congratulations! (*He makes eye contact again, once again shakes Jose's hand, and pats him on the back.*) Is it a boy or a girl?

José: A boy. I really need my job now. I hope there's nothing wrong with my work.

Antonio: Your performance is fine. I wanted to share with you that we're falling behind our new-accounts target goals for this year. That's why I need as many people as possible to work overtime.

José: I try hard to contribute despite my schedule. I've heard a lot of people are working overtime.

Antonio: Actually, I need everybody's help right now.

José: I'm going to night school, but I can probably change my schedule since the semester just started two weeks ago. I'll be very happy to help the bank. My wife will understand. However, I will need to go back to a regular schedule for at least a month after the baby is born. You understand my family comes first.

Antonio: That would be great. You're a real team player, my friend. Please tell your wife I appreciate her understanding—and let me know when the baby arrives. (*He makes eye contact and pats José's shoulder as he shakes his hand firmly and smiles.*)

Cultural Pointers

- Antonio uses direct communication with Michael to request his availability.
- Michael speaks in an individualistic manner and offers no information about his personal situation.
- Antonio and Michael talk only about work-related topics and reach an agreement.
- Antonio shows a caring attitude toward José's family in order to ease the tension that he sees reflected on José's face from the moment he walks into the office.
- When Antonio speaks to José, he appeals on behalf of the bank (group). The Latino collectivist approach helps him to enlist José's assistance.
- José avoids addressing the fact that he's not working overtime by adopting a passive stance as an outside observer ("I've heard a lot of people are working overtime").
- Antonio talks about *sharing* information with José instead of just informing him of the facts. José, in turn, welcomes Antonio's attitude. For Latinos, sharing denotes adherence to collectivism, a value that is as important as familism.
- As his supervisor, Antonio could simply ask José to work overtime. Instead, he leads José to volunteer. This indirect approach is successful, and José's response is very positive.
- Although José volunteers to help, he will need to put his family first once the baby arrives, so he has indicated beforehand that for one

month he will not be able to support his boss by working an extended schedule.

➤ Antonio uses a closer interpersonal distance, makes eye contact, shakes hands, and pats José on the shoulder to establish culturally appropriate communication.

SPANISH IN THE WORKPLACE

In a professional business setting, Latinos speak English because it is the universal language of business. At work, Latinos communicate in English with mainstream American peers. However, variations exist in the way Latinos of different generations communicate among themselves in the workplace.

First-generation immigrant Latinos may feel they can express ideas more clearly and feel more comfortable speaking Spanish, so they will almost automatically speak their own language with other Latinos. They do not mean to be rude; they are simply thinking and talking in the manner that comes most naturally, just as a group of Americans working as expatriates in, say, Germany will most likely speak English when they are together—it would be unnatural for them to speak in German. While shopping for office supplies recently, I (Nilda) realized that the saleswoman was a Spanish-speaker, so I switched to Spanish. Her sigh of relief was instant as she said, 'Why are we wasting our English between ourselves! Let's save it for our conversations with those who don't speak Spanish!"

When English-proficient immigrant Latinos incorporate Spanish words into their conversations, it may be that they are using Spanish words for which there is no exact English translation. Or they may perceive that the English translation of a Spanish word does not express the precise cultural nuances they are looking for. A friend recently told me (Nilda) that he could not understand how English speakers could live with having a single word to express such a complex feeling as "love." Interestingly, he said, Spanish has more than 25 words that mean *love*.

Second- and sometimes even third- and fourth-generation Latinos, too, often interject Spanish words into a conversation in English. For them, this may be a way of making use of the best words from both languages, as well as an expression of pride in their Latino heritage. My (Nilda's) niece and nephew are second generation and mainstream. They often use *Spanglish*, a combination of English and Spanish, because they are proud to let relatives know that they do know some Spanish. If pressed, however, they cannot engage in an entire conversation in Spanish.

What Do Latinos Mean When They Speak Spanish at Work? It is likely that Latinos are not trying to make a statement by speaking Spanish at work, but simply feel more at ease speaking in their own language. They are probably not even talking about work or about non-Spanish-speaking peers, but if they are, they are generally discussing concerns with the intention of resolving issues. It is not easy for Latinos to confront others with negative comments; when they do, they prefer to consult with people they trust—in this case, other Latinos who are part of their network in the workplace. Ironically, from their perspective, the use of Spanish allows them to be diplomatic and maintain good relationships.

How Do Mainstream Americans Interpret a Group of Latinos Speaking Spanish? Non–Spanish speakers are likely to perceive Latinos speaking Spanish in the workplace as rude and inappropriate. This behavior may give the impression that Latinos want to leave others out of the conversation or that they are talking about the non–Spanish speakers. Often, as noted above, that is not the case.

Some Latinos have had similar experiences in their home countries in the past. They are used to hearing U.S. Americans speak English among themselves while visiting Latin America on business, but they do not consider it rude, nor do they resent it. They simply respect U.S. Americans' language preference and understand that, because of lack of fluency in Spanish, English is their preferred language of communication.

How can the problem of suspicion and resentment be dealt with in the workplace? Unless the issue has been brought up because of a specific situation, Latinos are generally unaware of any suspicion or resentment regarding their use of Spanish. Once they become aware of it, they will readily use English, but only because of the importance they place on having harmonious relationships.

There are several ways to deal with this issue. Some organizations have language policies in place; others do not. Regardless, anyone who feels uncomfortable with the use of Spanish because it is not understood by everyone in a group should let Latinos know. A single comment is often sufficient to encourage Latinos to discontinue the practice. If there are reasons to believe that Latinos may be speaking about concerns related to their performance or jobs, it is best to ask them directly to discuss the issues openly. *Latinos will likely hold on to their ideas until asked to share them.* Once asked, however, they will often volunteer their thoughts, and they will be careful in the way they express them because they give priority to avoiding confrontations and maintaining harmonious relations with peers.

The vignettes that follow will illustrate two common situations in which Latinos speak Spanish at work.

VIGNETTE

෨෨ Michelle Jackson works as an office manager at the legal offices of James and James. Her staff consists of eight paralegals and two administrative assistants. Lately she has noticed some tension between her Latino employees and the others, who are mostly mainstream and Asian. On Friday morning, one of her mainstream employees, Joel, comes to Michelle's office and asks to speak with her. He complains that Alberto, Iris, and Esteban have a habit of speaking in Spanish in the kitchenette when they take their lunch break. He shares that the rest of the group, who also have lunch in the same place, believe that the Spanish speakers are talking about them.

At her next staff meeting, Michelle brings up the issue and asks everyone to participate.

Michelle Jackson: Some of you have mentioned that you have issues regarding Spanish being spoken during lunchtime in the kitchenette. I'd like to hear your thoughts on this.

Iris: Well, Alberto, Esteban, and I often speak in Spanish when we're together, so there's no doubt that whoever made the comment is referring to us.

Joel: I made the comment, Iris. It can get annoying sometimes.

Alberto: I had no idea you guys were even aware of it.

Esteban: I didn't know you cared what language we use when we're having lunch. In my view, it's our business.

Joel: Well, you're right. It *is* your business—as long as you keep it to yourselves. But the rest of us are also there hearing you all laugh and talk in Spanish.

Mary: I sometimes wonder if Iris is talking about me.

Iris: What makes you think something like that? Why would I talk about you, Mary?

Mary: I don't know. It's just a thought that crosses my mind sometimes, since you and I are the two administrative assistants here.

Iris: Let me assure you that I'm not talking about you.

Mary: I'm glad to know that, Iris. Thanks for saying it.

Joel: You guys are always laughing. What are you laughing about?

Esteban: You're probably going to think it's silly. Most of the time we're telling jokes that we've heard at home when we get together with our families on weekends.

Joel: So that's why you laugh so hard!

Alberto: Listen, if it is a problem for everyone else, we can stop doing it. We don't intend to create any problems. We like you all.

Mary: Thank you, Alberto. I, for one, appreciate the offer.

Joel: Well, I'd like to hear your jokes. Judging from how much you seem to enjoy them, they're probably pretty good.

Iris: You know, I've never translated jokes from Spanish into in English. I don't know if they will be so funny in English.

Esteban: If you want to hear them, we can give it a try.

Joel: I suggest that we start at lunch today!

Michelle: I think that's a great idea!

Cultural Pointers

- Joel was assertive; he approached his manager to present the issue that concerned him and the rest of the staff who were being affected by it.
- Michelle understands that in the multicultural environment at the office, she must act as a facilitator so that her staff can discuss and resolve the situation.
- Iris let everyone know that she was not talking about Mary. That cleared the way to discussing the issue of the Latino employees laughing while they were speaking in Spanish.
- After the three Latinos expressed to the group that they were willing to stop speaking Spanish and reassured everyone that they had not intended to create an uncomfortable atmosphere, everyone relaxed. The Latinos wanted to be in harmony with their peers.
- When Joel invited Iris, Esteban, and Alberto to share their jokes, the situation became one in which all could share. They moved toward a collectivist style of interaction.

VIGNETTE

The following vignette is a conversation between Rebeca Santiago, Mariana Hernández, and Jennifer Malcolm, who all work in a retail store selling children's clothing. Jennifer supervises both of the others, and they are discussing their language strategy with the clients. Although Rebeca and Mariana are Latinas, their Spanish-language proficiency is different. Mariana is fluent in both languages, whereas Rebeca does not like to speak Spanish, largely because she does not feel fully proficient in the language.

Jennifer Malcolm: I wanted to have a conversation with both of you, because we need to increase our sales. As you know, we operate in a largely Latino neighborhood, and speaking Spanish will be critical to accomplishing this. Among all of our staff, you are the only two Spanish speakers, and I expect you play a critical role.

Mariana Hernández: Well, that's fine with me. I feel comfortable in both languages, and once the client and I recognize each other as Latinas, we immediately switch to Spanish.

Jennifer: Good. I will let the other employees know to refer anyone to you who does not feel comfortable in English. How about you, Rebeca? I've noticed that you always speak to clients in English.

Rebeca Santiago: Well, I can speak some Spanish, but frankly I prefer not to—it feels uncomfortable. I was born in the U.S. and although my parents spoke Spanish at home, we always got away with responding in English. I have a heavy gringo accent and I'm afraid the clients will make fun of me.

Jennifer: I understand how you feel, but you probably know that clients would be happier to hear some words in their own language even if you are not fully fluent.

Rebeca: I do, but I also want to make sure that I'm giving them the right price and the right information about what they are buying.

Mariana: Listen, *mi amiga* [my friend], if you know some Spanish, you might as well use it.

Jennifer: Mariana has a point. You'll help them feel comfortable, and you'll make the sale.

Rebeca: I see your point, but when I say a few words in Spanish, some clients get loud and all speak at the same time. That makes it more difficult to understand. If I speak in English, I am in full control of the situation.

Mariana: Well, you know that we tend to be enthusiastic and playful when we speak Spanish, so it's not just a matter of knowing the language. It's also a matter of being patient and enjoying being Latina.

Rebeca: Well, it can't hurt. I'll give it a try.

Jennifer: I appreciate it. With both of you supporting us with the language issue, we should be successful in meeting our sales goals.

Cultural Pointers

- Spanish is becoming an essential skill in many work environments because of the large number of immigrant and Spanish-speaking Latinos living in the U.S.
- People will always appreciate hearing some words in their native language, even if the person giving the information is not fully proficient in Spanish.
- Many second-, third-, and fourth-generation Latinos do not feel comfortable speaking Spanish.
- Mainstream supervisors may be under the impression that all Latinos are fluent in Spanish, but some may actually fall short in these skills. If Spanish-language fluency is stated as a requirement in the job description, we highly recommend that the Latino candidate's level of proficiency be tested.
- When Mariana uses a few Spanish words in her conversation with Rebeca, she is not trying to leave the mainstream supervisor out of the loop, she is trying to emphasize her bond with Rebeca as a fellow Latina and, in this way, to encourage Rebeca to use Spanish.

Gender Issues in the Workplace

Yolanda was born in the United States. Her Latino parents, who emigrated from a Spanish-speaking Caribbean country, understood that Yolanda would become bicultural and bilingual because she was growing up in a mainstream environment. They made special efforts to expose Yolanda to their cultural ways. Her father still works; her mother, who has never worked outside the home, baby-sits for relatives' and friends' children at her house.

Yolanda's first language is English; she speaks Spanish with an accent. Her mother, to this day, does not speak English very well, so she cannot communicate with Yolanda in anything but Spanish. Yolanda studied advertising and currently works for a global firm. She met Javier, her Latino husband, at the university. Javier is a first-generation immigrant from Honduras who arrived in the United States to get his M.B.A. Upon completion of his degree, he married Yolanda and settled down in the U.S. They have two young children, who don't like to speak Spanish, although they do understand it.

Javier works as the administrator for a medium-size trade company dealing with Latin America and Europe. His family is in Central America, and he sees them twice a year. He and his wife and children visit his parents at Christmas, and his parents come to the U.S. during the summer.

Yolanda's children go to school by bus. Before going to the office, Yolanda stops at the gym for a workout, then takes a conference call with her supervisee from her car. A big client is coming in today. Javier leaves for work later because he needs to wait for the housekeeper who comes three times a week. He's learned to incorporate some mainstream ways in his life, so he does some cooking and helps with the chores when he's not at work. His schedule is flexible; he starts work from home, reading and responding to his e-mail and phoning several clients in Europe, where the time is quite a few hours ahead. Today, Javier is concerned because he has a Latino employee who is going through difficult personal times with a sick family member; Javier knows he'll need to give this employee special attention.

From Javier and Yolanda's morning routine, it might not be obvious that they are not mainstream until you hear them speak Spanish and see their Latino presence. Increasingly, many Latino employees are similar to Yolanda and Javier. Their household reflects a mix of Latino and mainstream cultures. For example, Yolanda, unlike her own mother, works outside the home; today, more than 50 percent of Latinas work full-time (Cresce 1992). Men like Javier are often no longer the sole providers because their spouses contribute an important part of the family income. Finally, men are not the only ones who supervise, as more Latinas accept managerial positions. Yolanda has people working for her, just as Javier does.

This shift results from an increase in financial needs, professional aspirations, and degree of acculturation. This chapter will describe the different ways in which gender issues affect Latinos in the workplace. We will use Yolanda, Javier, and their parents to illustrate our points regarding *machismo* and *marianismo*, two values that strongly influence Latino behavior.

MACHISMO

The term *machismo* refers to the expectation in Latino culture that men will assume the dominant position in relationships (Mayo 1997). In most Latino families, men hold positions of authority; the exceptions are families headed by single mothers. The way Latino culture treats males at home affects their behavior and their perception of their gender roles and authority at work. It is likely that we may find stronger evidence of machismo in Yolanda's and Javier's fathers than we do in Javier himself. Javier helps with chores at homes, has no problem with Yolanda working independently outside the house, and, in general, does not consider himself the center of the universe.

The Providers and Protectors   Latino men often perceive their role as that of providers and protectors in both family and work. Such is the case for Yolanda and Javier's parents: only the men work outside the home, and most such men likely take great pride in reasonably covering their family needs. Although Yolanda's mother baby-sits, she does this in her own home.

Male income seems to carry heavier weight in the Latino household, regardless of the amount. The husband's salary is considered more important and tends to be used first and foremost for basic needs, such as food, school, and mortgage payments.

Many Latino men continue to see themselves in a central role despite the fact that women are increasingly becoming important breadwinners. Even females who have a higher salary than their husbands would not likely handle their finances separately but would place all of the household income in a joint account. In many cases, the male will play a preponderant role in the distribution of the money. This is not necessarily because he is more financially savvy than his wife, but because Latinas tend to let the man feel that he is in control. Women play an influential role, but they do so in a subtle way, without making their husbands feel diminished, which would hurt their self-esteem and affect the relationship.

This is due in part to the fact that both husband and wife have a sense of pride when the man is able to provide for the family. This indicates that the woman has chosen a husband who is a good protector, a hard-working man who thinks of his family first. If this is the case, the wife can work at whatever she likes, without financial pressure. Even if the wife works and contributes to the household, recognition of the husband's effort is very important to both of them.

Some managers brought up in traditional Latino families who supervise female workers may still consider that the woman's place is in the
home. They may wonder about the motivation of working females or
about their husbands' manliness and ability to provide. Part of the Latino
male's status, especially for one who is culturally traditional, is having a
stay-at-home wife. Older Latinas will likely have limited work experience,
primarily in administrative positions. This is the case with Javier's and
Yolanda's mothers. By contrast, Javier met Yolanda in an academic environment, indicating that Yolanda's intention was to be professionally
independent.

The *machista* attitude may, at times, bias a traditional Latino male
supervisor when making decisions regarding women employees. He may
believe that a woman's salary will be used for personal luxuries rather
than to cover household needs. If her reason for working outside the
home is to procure money for her own purposes, then her husband will
not be judged negatively. Thus, when granting salary increases, some traditional Latino supervisors may feel that a man has needs above and
beyond those of his female employees.

An example of a machista attitude is exemplified in a situation I
(Francia) witnessed a few years ago involving a Latino supervisor and his
two Latino supervisees, one male and one female. As a result of an internal reorganization combining two formerly separate divisions, the scope
of these two employees' jobs increased. Both were assigned similar
responsibilities overseeing identical populations, each in their area of
specialization. The man was discreetly promoted; the woman was not.
When I mentioned this fact to the supervisor, he responded with many
reasons that indicated that he believed he was doing the right thing. In his
view, the man had been in his position longer, would supervise a more
complex subject, and was more experienced than the woman. Further, he
believed that the man's role was greater and warranted recognition. It
probably never occurred to him that he was not evaluating both employees using the same criteria. The Latina he supervised never approached
him with her concerns, and he never gave her an explanation. She was not
even given a salary increase in recognition of her added responsibilities.

This story reflects a machista attitude, a male behavior that gives men a preeminent position as leaders, providers, and protectors. In this view, men make the decisions, establish the goals, own the truth, possess knowledge, and, above all, help one another. After all, who can better understand a man and his responsibilities than another man? In sharp contrast, this attitude minimizes the role of women.

Paternalism Paternalism—looking after employees' social and material concerns—is a common practice in Latin America (Warner 2002). The Latino supervisor may feel a sense of paternalism when making work-related decisions, such as salary increases, bonuses, and providing for employees' needs, regardless of the gender of the employee. Latino males have been taught to play this role at home, and thus it is the one that they believe will gain them approval in the workplace.

Such is Javier's case today with the employee who has a sick family member. He will discuss the situation with the employee, identify ways of supporting him, and suggest that the employee take advantage of the Family and Medical Leave Act (FMLA) to allow him to take some free time at home to care for the relative. The employee has told Javier that he is having difficulties, but, as a Latino supervisor, Javier already knows that it is his duty to protect the workers he supervises.

The paternalistic attitude exhibited by some Latino supervisors may reach supervisees and may extend to family members and cover situations both within and outside of the work environment. Latino supervisors may feel responsible for employees' physical, mental, and emotional well-being. This supervisor will likely expect the employee to approach him or her in a time of need. In fact, not asking the supervisor for help may create tension in the relationship. A supervisor may say, "Why didn't you come to me? That's what I'm here for" or "Hey, we're supposed to be like family." The Latino supervisor needs the opportunity to carry out his or her role and show a caring attitude.

An unwritten Latino norm states that if you are blessed with prosperity, your obligation is to be grateful and to show it by sharing your wealth with others. Supervisors are individuals who have received recognition and status in their careers; therefore, they must honor this norm. My (Francia's) parents are Latinos; for them, owning a house and ensuring that their children have a good education are vital goals. My father, in his multiple public office positions, and my mother (with the household staff) both exhibited paternalism in their working relationships. My father negotiated housing plans for his employees with various government agencies, and the down payment for the housekeepers' homes generally came from our savings. As the school year approached, my home must have resembled a brokerage office, as my parents went about identifying scholarship opportunities for the children of their staffs. Everyone who worked for them needed to meet those goals, and my parents were the facilitators responsible for making this happen. Needless to say, the same process occurred for family members and friends in need.

The machista supervisor may believe that the role of women as mothers and wives hampers their ability to perform their professional duties. In this way, Latino supervisors may be paternalistic in protecting women even from themselves. They rationalize this attitude as follows: *How are these mothers going to come to work if the child has a fever? What is going to happen to those children after school if the mother is not there for them?* Therefore, do not be surprised if a traditional Latino indicates that he would really prefer to have a man as employee because men do not give birth and do not need to care for children. In the Latino environment, the idea of a stay-at-home father—a practice that is becoming common in the U.S.—is still a very questionable matter.

It's not uncommon to hear negative comments among Latinos regarding working mothers whose children become involved with drugs, sex, or alcohol. "Oh, no wonder," they may say. "She worked, so the kids were alone at home." The judgmental statement does not take into account that these problems may happen to the children of stay-at-home mothers as well. Often the traditional Latino male may disregard the professional aspirations of Latinas, who are expected to carry out their duty and raise the children, so professional progress and travel may interfere with the assignment of tasks at home. Surely many of Javier's relatives can't understand why he stays at home if the children are sick or why he needs to wait for the housekeeper while Yolanda goes off to the gym.

Although it can be difficult for Latinos to eradicate machismo from work-related decisions, the attitude toward women is gradually changing as a result of Latinas' increased work responsibilities and stronger participation in managing the household finances. In many cases, the unfortunate increase in the number of single Latina mothers or divorcées has forced these women to be the sole financial providers for the household. Together with those married Latinas with professional aspirations, there are increasing numbers of women who work and who are willing to carry out whatever duties are required in their professional roles.

Even in Latin American countries, when a company asks colleges and universities to send their best students for interviews, a large majority of these students are likely to be women, proving the interest and discipline of Latinas who are breaking through cultural barriers in terms of their own academic preparation for the future.

VIGNETTE

෧෨ Eladio Martinez, Yolanda's father, is a supervisor in a large computer company. He immigrated to the United States 30 years ago and knows how to navigate the mainstream culture fairly well, but he continues to exhibit Latino cultural behavior at work. Eladio's machista attitude has caused some friction with female supervisees. This vignette captures his conversation regarding a new franchise, with Cesar, one of his employees, who is also having difficulty with his wife. Cesar is also Latino. He is in his late forties and arrived in the U.S. a couple of years ago. Both Cesar and his wife work outside the house, more out of financial need than out of Cesar's wish for his wife to fulfill her professional aspirations.

Eladio Martínez: Hi, Cesar. How are you doing?
Cesar: I'm OK, Eladio. By the way, I really enjoyed our outing last
    week. Man, we had fun at that bar! My wife was not too happy

when I got home. You know, she thinks she can boss me around because she brings in money. But she's wrong, because I'm still the man of the house. She sends some of her salary back home to her mom and then she uses what's left for all of her little wishes. But me—I bring in the hard cash.

Do you know what she used part of her salary for last month? A massage and a day at a spa, because she needed to "get away from it all"! She knows she can't use my money for that.

Eladio: Yeah, I know what you mean. I had trouble at first, too, but my wife can't complain. I work for both of us, and that gives her a chance to stay at home. I know she once wanted to work, but what for? Financially we don't need it. Professionally, I don't see the benefit. She baby-sits at home, and that takes up most of her time. She's used to it by now. She knows I take care of everything, so I decide what to do with time, money, and family.

Cesar: That's good thinking, Eladio. I could use some of your ideas to handle my situation. What's worked for you?

Eladio: What's worked for me is staying in control and doing what I've been taught to do. Let her feel your authority, but blend it in with some balance. I have my night out with you guys, but I also find time for the grandkid's stuff at school, and I'm there when the family needs me.

Cesar: Interesting. I'll think about it.

Eladio: By the way, I have to talk to you about the new franchise we are opening in Central America. I think you may be able to help us get it established.

Cultural Pointers

- Although Eladio supervises Cesar, they also share social time after work. They combine personal and professional issues and talk about their private matters openly.
- Their conversation reflects their views about female roles at home and

in the workplace. It also covers their views on their own independence and their role as providers.

➤ As is common in a conversation between Latinos, they take care of the personal before they go to business matters. In this case, they discuss the reactions of their wives to their last night out and their views on women working before focusing on the new franchise expansion.

MARIANISMO

Marianismo is a socially learned female behavior among Latinas whereby they perform duties as nurturers to husband and children. This concept presents the Virgin Mary as a model for expectations of the female role. The link is so strong that the worshipers of the Virgin Mary are called Marianos. Thus, women are expected to show all of the Virgin Mary's attributes. Expectations include purity, chastity, fidelity, and obedience; focus on house and children; respect; and letting the men in their lives (father and husband) control their destiny.

A second- or third-generation Latina today may still exhibit many of these attributes but will combine them with an active role in her own education and career. Most also have a different perspective on their relationship with men at home and men at work. Their interest in working outside the home comes largely from a need to contribute to the family income in order to procure more and better things for the family. However, it also includes a personal interest in professional fulfillment and testing their own capabilities.

Many Latinas today seem to prepare better than in the past to face the challenges of the corporate work environment. Thus, although their incomes may be lower than those of their male colleagues, they may still earn as much as or more than their own husbands do. If this is the case, they will likely downplay this fact in order to protect the man's image and to maintain harmony at home.

In the past, wives were expected to stay at home and trust in the men in their lives to take care of everything, but this is no longer enough for their daughters. Latinas are taking charge of their finances, balancing their own checking accounts, and making spending decisions. Even their fathers are now encouraging them to become academically and professionally accomplished, often emphasizing the fact that reaching higher educational levels will allow them to achieve personal success and financial freedom.

Even as Latinas pursue higher education and professional careers, Latino views about the roles of men and women in the household continue to affect the way many Latinas relate to the inevitable conflicts that arise between home and work. Many Latino men do not get involved with household chores, even if the wife works. My (Francia's) parents, for example, took great pride in mentioning that before we immigrated to the U.S., my father did not know the color his kitchen was painted. For him, this meant that he was busy working hard, that he had limited time for household activities, and that he was successful enough to have a maid to help at home. Why would he go into the kitchen? I would not be surprised to find a similar situation with Javier's parents, who still live in Latin America, although it is likely that Yolanda's immigrant father had to adapt to more involvement in the household, just as mine did.

Whether or not it corresponds to reality, in the Latino image of mainstream culture, all family members are expected to participate in household responsibilities. Thus, Javier actively helps out with household chores—even though he and Yolanda have a part-time housekeeper—and both Yolanda and Javier are comfortable with this arrangement.

Working Latinas feel responsible for marriage, children, and household chores as part of their socially defined role. Their work outside of the home is not expected to interfere with their responsibility as nurturers for the family. If a conflict arises, it is the career that must be sacrificed, because family is the focus of women's lives. Thus, many Latina professionals prefer to stay home during their children's early years, although they may return to work later.

It still shocks me (Francia) to remember a colleague who, though of Latino origin, had been raised on one of the English-speaking Caribbean islands, so she had a mixed cultural background. To understand this case, it is important to know that in Latin America, pediatricians are more likely than those in the U.S. to use hospital stays for children as a sort of preventive medicine, in the belief that a sick child will recuperate faster in the hospital. So, when this colleague had sick children in the hospital, she would calmly arrange for supervision while she came to work. I respected her decision, but my own supervisor would have had to drag me with a bulldozer from my children's hospital bedside, even if the illness was not serious. Considering that I had both grandmothers, an aunt, and three cousins all sitting in a small hospital room at the same time, I probably could have taken off a few hours to catch up at the office. But I would have felt I was not fulfilling my role as a mother, and I was willing to sacrifice my career for my children. I am a dedicated and hardworking professional—as long as it doesn't interfere with my being a mother.

In my first job, I (Francia) can recall the supervisor indicating that he needed "a man with a mustache" (implying a "real" man) to perform peer reviews, so he gave this opportunity to someone else. I had been taught to wait patiently for my assignments instead of requesting the tasks that interested me, even if I knew I could perform more efficiently than my male colleague. Speaking up would have been seen as showing a lack of respect toward the supervisor, whom I looked up to. I would also have had to explain at home why I had volunteered for a task that would involve extensive travel alone, which would mean exposing myself to criticism and possibly uncomfortable situations. My supervisor, in turn, was simply reflecting his own upbringing and his desire to protect me. It was not a matter of my qualifications; he just thought he needed a man to do the job.

Latinas are taught to have respect for authority. Therefore, they will tend to keep their place at work, efficiently doing what is asked of them. They may even exceed themselves, but only within a limited scope. This show of power distance includes parents, teachers, and husbands as well as supervisors. As Todd (2001) notes, "Women in some Latino countries are raised not to look directly into the eye of a superior, whether the person is female or male. And many are taught not to bring up issues or questions that may draw attention to them. With this in mind, employers may have to work at getting feedback from their employees."

Some Latinas will likely not negotiate a higher salary and will make fewer demands concerning work conditions than a mainstream woman because of her typically subdued and less aggressive style. This style does not necessarily reflect Latinas' effectiveness at work or their level of discipline in getting things done. But it does affect the way they deal with supervisors and others in authority.

The interaction in the following vignette illustrates marianismo in the workplace.

VIGNETTE

෧෮ Eladio Martínez, whom we met while discussing machismo, is speaking with Antonia, who also reports to him. She is a Latina immigrant who arrived in the U.S. five years ago, with work experience and knowledge of the English language. She has three children and is managing to be successful both at work and at home.

> *Eladio Martínez:* Hi, Antonia. You're looking really nice today. I must say that you are one of the prettiest ladies in this company.
> *Antonia:* Thank you, Eladio.
> *Eladio:* You know what, I've always been surprised that your husband lets you work outside the house.
> *Antonia:* Oh, he is an excellent provider, Eladio. We don't really need my salary for the regular household expenses. I work because I have responsibilities for my brothers and sisters back home, and so I have to generate some income to send them.
> *Eladio:* It must be burdensome for you to have to do the chores at home every day after work. I don't know how you handle it.
> *Antonia:* Well, I'm happy with my job. I try to balance my time between my duties as a wife and mother, but I'm always responsible with my work.

Eladio: But you could have chosen a part-time or easier job. Why this complex and demanding role?

Antonia: Well, on the professional side, I like to prove myself. Selling computers is not traditional for a female, least of all for a Latina. But I have maintained the same workload as the men, and I have gained credibility with my staff and respect from my clients.

Eladio: I do recognize you for that. To be honest, Antonia, I thought you were not going to make it. You have proved me wrong, and you've done it without bothering me all the time about your compensation.

Antonia: And I never will. I work hard for my salary, and I have to trust that you make your decisions wisely. My work should speak for itself, and hopefully salary increases, schedule changes, or good assignments will follow. I take them as they come and just try to focus on my job.

Eladio: I want you to know that I'm here for you if you need anything, like time for your kids or your family responsibilities.

Antonia: Thanks, Eladio. I hope I don't have to take you at your word, but if I do, I will appreciate your support.

Eladio: I know, Antonia. Now, let me talk to you about a new franchise we are opening up in Latin America. I think that, with your perspective, you will be able to contribute.

Cultural Pointers

- Antonia represents the modern Latina with professional aspirations. She is trying to find her place in a corporation while maintaining her responsibilities at home.
- Eladio uses flattery to set a positive stage for the conversation. This should not be understood as an attempt to express physical attraction.
- Antonia acknowledges the flattery graciously, then steers the conversation away from it with an evasive "thank-you." Although she is confident of Eladio's respect, Latinas don't mind a few compliments but generally feel uncomfortable with a prolonged conversation of this nature.

- Although he respects Antonia's professionalism, Eladio shares his thoughts about husbands who allow their wives to work. Antonia excuses her husband, assuring her boss that her husband is a good provider.
- Eladio is still surprised that with so many other, less demanding jobs available, Antonia has chosen one that requires a lot from her, and in which she competes with male colleagues. He seems to think that she should have looked for something less challenging.
- Antonia thinks she will eventually get what she deserves professionally, so she is not focused on salary, work conditions, or recognition. It's not that she has no aspirations in these areas, but she has not been taught to negotiate for them. Rather, she has been taught to work hard and to accept what she gets in return. She may rebel internally in her hope of gaining more recognition, but it's unlikely she will do anything about it.
- Antonia is very clear about the respective place of family and work in her life. Work comes first as long as there is no need for her at home. The need for her to focus on the home kicks in regularly at a certain time every day, when she must get home to be there for the children and to prepare dinner. It also kicks in whenever a family emergency arises.

WORK INTERACTION AMONG MEN AND WOMEN

Relationships—a sense of the group or the community—are very important to Latinos. That is why so many people come together for every event—family, colleagues, friends, and more. Everyone becomes part of a close-knit group, and this closeness makes us feel like family—a feeling that is demonstrated physically through hugs, kisses, and touch. It is also demonstrated in support, comfort, and caring.

Latinos may not distinguish sharply between social and work behavior. This cultural characteristic can create confusion in the work environment. Latinos feel a sense of wholeness about the different settings in their lives, as compared to other cultural groups, for whom personal life may be kept private and may differ from their life at work.

There are strong cultural distinctions in the way Latinos react to gender issues. Latino males are likely to adopt the role of protector for female workers, in response to their own cultural orientation. This tendency becomes stronger when the male colleague and the husband of the female employee know each other, in which case the protective Latino also becomes a caring companion. When traveling for work, for example, he will rent the car and drive, while the female colleague, if she wishes, may take a passive attitude as passenger.

Relationships Latinos have strong, close relationships, even between men and women. However, Latino men and women are not usually alone in social interactions. That is, male and female colleagues would not likely go to a happy hour together. They may meet there with a group, but they would not go alone. This behavior would only occur in an atmosphere of intimacy. These same standards of behavior tend to apply to the work environment, where great care is taken to protect the female's image and the reputations of both families. In Latino culture, a woman can be misjudged for having too close a relationship with a male colleague, and such a relationship would likely lead to gossip that they were having an affair. A Latino man, however, is not concerned about his own reputation, because many grew up to believe that, as the saying goes, "*El hombre es de la calle*" ("The man belongs to the street"), meaning that men can go out and do as they please.

Female participation at work in the mainstream culture stresses equality. If a person's work typically calls for travel, attending a happy hour, or working late hours, he or she is expected to comply, regardless of gender. In more traditional settings or among more reserved Latinos, however, there may be some family struggle concerning the appropriateness of these activities. At the extreme, if a Latina cannot reach agreement at home to participate in these events, she may resign. A sensitive supervisor would want to inquire if a Latina employee is able to travel and spend long hours at work, to ensure adequate planning of activities and resources.

Gender in Supervisors As a result of machismo and marianismo, traditional Latinos may tend to resent having female supervisors. Some males may protest that not only did they not get the positions themselves, but also that they now have to report to a woman.

Although a male commands almost instantaneous credibility and trust, a female in an executive role must prove she is worthy of the position. Know-how, experience, and performance do not grant her immediate acceptance as the right person for the job. Rather, she will have to win that acceptance. This feeling is the same regardless of the female supervisor's cultural background, although a Latina may have an more difficult time being accepted.

In one of my (Francia's) previous jobs, we conducted a series of customer round-table discussions. At the end of the sessions, the consultant we had hired asked the participants, in a lighthearted spirit, to describe the typical high-ranking employee of a domestic public-sector organization, a private company, and a foreign organization.

The clients, who were all Latino, indicated that the employee in the public sector got his position through *amiguismo,* a Spanish term indicating that one gets ahead by being someone's friend. They also pointed out that this person would generally be male, typically not very competent, and would lead in a very unstructured way.

For the domestic private company, they described the typical high-ranking employee as a man with a house at the beach, a driver, a large house in the city, and an extensive domestic staff to help. They indicated that this person had most likely benefited from amiguismo in getting the job in the first place, but that he would have a college degree and a reasonable level of competence.

Interestingly, the high-ranking officer for the foreign organization was described as female, highly competent in her work, very professional, and possibly with a graduate degree earned in the United States. She was seen as having gotten her job on her own merits; if there was any form of intervention, it was just an introduction. She would likely live in an apartment, be very efficient in balancing family and work, and have a lifestyle resembling that of a U.S. American.

These hypothetical employees, of course, were not created on the basis of scientific research, but they do give us a flavor of how Latinos view different managerial profiles and how they might accept women in positions of power if the organization is not domestic.

In an environment with a large Latino workforce, a female supervisor may need to project strong leadership skills to prevent harsh treatment from male subordinates. She will probably have to come across as tough, so that the males will feel confident that she can be as tough as they are. It is not uncommon to hear of men placing bets on how long a female supervisor will last on the job. Latinas who attain executive positions may need to struggle harder than their male counterparts to establish their place with other Latino employees.

However, once the Latina supervisor has withstood the initial test and is seen as having proved her worth, most Latino employees will expect her to provide for and protect them in the same manner as a male supervisor would. These behavioral expectations seem more intrinsic to the supervisory role than they are gender-specific.

WORK INTERACTION AMONG LATINAS

Latinas tend to develop strong bonds at work. They spend a substantial amount of time together, so a sense of closeness evolves naturally. They will provide support to one another, help out with a task, teach a skill, and so on. There is a natural protectiveness among them, and a sense of *sisterhood* is likely to develop.

This feeling of sisterhood implies that these Latinas will protect, motivate, and support one another in their tasks and needs. It can also imply personal and social interaction. Their families may spend time together, especially when the children are small, although husbands will not necessarily participate in their wives' work relationships.

Latinas tend to socialize actively in the work environment. They generally have opinions on many subjects and always welcome an opportunity to comment. At times, this ready expression of opinions about people and events may be seen as gossip. Latinas also tend to mix the professional and the personal. Thus, they may discuss personal events in their lives at work and also discuss work events outside of the professional setting.

Latinas who reach high levels within an organization are likely to bring in other women and to give them opportunities for advancement as an investment in the future. When the supervisor and the employee are both women, their sense of sisterhood will give them a better chance to focus on the job and not get distracted by trying to prove themselves.

WORK INTERACTION AMONG MEN

Most Latinos tend to develop strong friendships with other males at work. They will generally share social activities with them, often including family members. This work-related interaction in a social setting creates an obligation for the family. As head of the household, the man assumes his wife will understand that her role is to support her husband's career and will follow his initiative when it comes to meeting socially with his workmates or supervisors. These activities outside work strengthen the ties among the male colleagues and allow for better professional relationships.

Latino colleagues may candidly share personal situations with one another while maintaining a reasonable professional distance in their work relationship. They treat professional boundaries with great respect. Nonetheless, they also expect that a colleague-turned-friend will become an ally and protector as the two men become part of the *brotherhood* that serves as a supportive network.

The use of language is relaxed among Latino males, who often share jokes and private comments among themselves. When respectful interactions across genders develop, some males may feel comfortable sharing racy jokes with Latinas, as well. This may seem highly inappropriate in the mainstream culture, where men would rarely share such jokes with women and would never do so in a work environment. Perhaps Latinos can get away with this because of the overall sense of respect, which is certainly defined differently than it is in the mainstream culture. The absence of such behavior in the mainstream culture may also be the result of the consciousness of the potential for sexual harassment issues to arise in the workplace. Further discussion of sexual harassment will be found in Chapter 9. The following vignette illustrates gender issues in the work environment.

VIGNETTE

೦ Yolanda, whom we met at the beginning of this chapter, discusses a work situation with a management associate she is mentoring. Mary, the associate, is mainstream. She was an intern in Yolanda's department; then, after she graduated from college, Yolanda recruited her. Mary is currently working with a male manager.

> *Mary:* Yolanda, I wanted to talk to you about a situation at work that has me worried.
>
> *Yolanda:* OK, Mary. What are you concerned about?
>
> *Mary:* Well, it's about relationships. When I was working for you, I felt a strong bond. You gave me opportunities to learn and exposed me to new situations. You let me be who I am professionally and personally.
>
> *Yolanda:* Developing your potential by allowing you to spread your wings is part of your training.
>
> *Mary:* I really enjoyed the experience, but now my manager, José, does not act the same way. He is overprotective with me and limits my assignments. I can't figure out why he does that.
>
> *Yolanda:* Give me some specific examples, so I can understand better.
>
> *Mary:* We were supposed to visit a client yesterday. In the days when we were preparing for the presentation, I felt like I was working for one of my parents. José ordered dinner at night; he made me go home by 9:00 P.M., even though we still had work and I was willing to stay. He even ordered a taxi for me! I usually take the train.
>
> *Yolanda:* I see. Anything else?
>
> *Mary:* Well, I really needed to convince him to give me that assignment in the first place; he wanted to give it to the two male associates in

the department. Finally, yesterday we drove to the client's office to make the presentation. I knew my way there because I had gone there before, but he wouldn't let me drive. He said he would be the driver. Although I had prepared to make the presentation to the clients, in the end, he did it and only allowed me to support him. We got the account, and then, in the evaluation meeting afterward, he acknowledged the team effort, which I felt in a way actually minimized my role, because 80 percent of the work was mine.

Yolanda: Mary, your boss, José, is Latino.

Mary: What do you mean?

Yolanda: His behavior may seem hard to understand, but it is very clear to another Latino.

Mary: Well, then I'm going to need an explanation.

Yolanda: You see, he views his relationship with women differently from a relationship with other men. From childhood, Latino males are taught to be protective of females. That's why he ordered dinner and got a cab for you; he wanted to make sure you got home safely. You were doing an assignment for him, so he would not tolerate your being unsafe because of him. The same applies to his driving to the meeting and his making the presentation. He has been taught to take that lead, especially when the person he is partnering with is a woman.

Mary: And it's not that I don't appreciate all his effort, Yolanda, because I do. But I feel very uncomfortable to be pampered that way at work. The way he treats me is different from how he treats my male colleagues. It just can't be good for my career!

Yolanda: José will not do anything to jeopardize your future, but he may have a harder time recognizing your potential when giving out an assignment. José works with women, but he still has some struggles recognizing that they are as competent and able as men. You did the right thing by approaching him to let him know you wanted that account. And he reacted rationally and gave it to you.

Mary: I really don't know if he values my work.

Yolanda: He recognizes how well you did. He even bragged about your performance at a meeting yesterday, and all he said was that he was so lucky to have you working for him.

Mary: So if he did recognize my skills and I prepared something so good that it won the client over, why did he talk about it as if it were a group effort?

Yolanda: Oh, it's very clear to me. It just means he sees the results as the participation of several people. Let's count the people involved: José, who gave you the assignment; you, who prepared the presentation; the secretary, who made the copies and put them in binders; the male associates, who focused on other tasks to allow you to concentrate on this one; and so forth. You see, there *was* a group effort there, and José will always feel he has ownership over the work of his subordinates.

Mary: Wow, that's a really different way of seeing this. It's not that I agree with it, but at least I understand where he is coming from and don't feel so bad anymore.

Cultural Pointers

- When Yolanda recruited Mary as an intern, she made efforts to ensure that Mary had opportunities to use her talent. Mary did not have to focus on trying to establish her space; rather, Yolanda did this for her so that she could concentrate on the actual assignments. In her current role as an associate, Mary needs to fight for her own space; she is busy trying to make others see her capabilities.

- José's actions are well intentioned. He sees potential in Mary and values her work, although he may not acknowledge it directly. He feels a responsibility to ensure that she is protected and that no harm comes to her if he can possibly prevent it. This makes Mary uncomfortable; she views this behavior as overprotective and believes that José's attitude minimizes her independence and capabilities.

- José is group-oriented, so it is hard for him to recognize Mary as the sole contributor to the assignment. He knows she carried most of the weight in this assignment, but in his view everyone contributed.
- By explaining José's likely motivations, Yolanda has opened Mary's eyes to a different cultural perspective.
- Jose's actions could lead to gender discrimination lawsuits and other workplace problems, but he is not aware of it. In his own mind, he is just trying to do his job well.

Understanding Latinos' Style at Work

The U.S. media, particularly the movie industry, may tend to present Latinos living in the United States as fitting into one of two stereotypical categories. In the first group are the poor, underprivileged immigrants who struggle and make sacrifices, day in and day out, simply to survive from paycheck to paycheck. These are many of the hardworking service employees and construction workers who may not speak English and who, in some cases, may be barely able to read or write in their own language. They are Jaime the gardener, José the barber, María the nanny. Some may bow their heads and may sometimes let the supervisors and mainstream peers take control while they quietly hide from the world—and perhaps from the immigration authorities as well. To many mainstream Americans, these Latinos' ways are so different from their own that the only perceived link between them may seem to be a few steps of salsa on the dance floor, an occasional taco, or perhaps knowing a few words in Spanish.

The second stereotype calls to mind the group honored in the title of the Latino singer Ricky Martin's song "Living la Vida Loca"—"living the crazy life." In this stereotypical image, Latinos may be portrayed as individuals involved with drugs and prostitution, or with smuggling illegal immigrants; or they may be gang members who steal from and assault strangers and family members alike.

Mainstream individuals who have infrequent contact with Latinos may be led to think that all Latinos fit into one of these two groups. In reality, individuals who fit these stereotypes are found in all cultural groups—they are not unique to Latinos. People in all cultures are a product not just of the values of their ethnic group but also of their individual personalities, environment, and upbringing. In sum, most Latinos do not fit either of these stereotypes.

Behind the scenes, largely ignored by the movies and other media, are most Latinos. You will not find them as characters in the movies or in newspaper stories about the hardships faced by undocumented immigrants. Rather, they are the ones behind the camera, filming or directing the movies, editing the newspaper stories, or planning the marketing strategy for movies, newspapers, and magazines. Many Latinos in the United States hold jobs in domestic and global organizations, large and small. They may have university degrees, may excel in their jobs, and may reach the senior executive level in a corporation or even start their own companies. Contrary to the stereotype of Latinos leading disorderly lives, most Latinos in the U.S. marry, have a limited number of children, take good care of their homes, and save money in order to achieve their aspirations. Someday they or their children will proudly call themselves American citizens. These Latinos contribute their cultural values to the mainstream work environment and to U.S. society.

As we have learned, Latinos are part of a distinct culture and thus may react differently than mainstream employees in many work situations. The cultural aspect of the Latino work style is also influenced by ethics, professional and academic attainment, work experience, and level of acculturation. This chapter presents a discussion of Latino responses to certain workplace dynamics that may challenge and influence their behavior. Understanding these responses will make it easier to comprehend Latino subordinates, peers, and supervisors.

MOTIVATION

What motivates people to get up every morning and start their work routine? People work for salary, of course. But how about other incentives? Are the motivations for a Latino worker different from those that drive a mainstream worker? An in-depth look at this issue reveals a mix of commonalities and differences.

The single most important motivator for Latinos is generally the family. Knowing that they have children or parents who need financial support helps Latinos face the daily routine. They will try to perform effectively in order to hold on to their jobs so that they can fulfill their family obligations. This motivation is especially strong among immigrants, for whom making it to the United States and getting a job here already imply personal and professional achievement. Thus, Latino immigrants, especially, feel an obligation to recognize all those who facilitated their successful transition and supported them along the way toward achieving their goals. Their success will not have the same significance if it is not shared, which they generally do by financially supporting relatives in their home country. Work, for Latino immigrants, is primarily a vehicle for obtaining the things their family needs—not the purpose of life itself. People talk about the difference between "working to live" and "living to work." The Latino way is to work to live, because providing for family always comes first.

As in other cultures, money is certainly a motivator. However, Latinos consider the mainstream culture somewhat more money-conscious than their own. They are focused less on money as a goal in itself than on the things that money can buy, starting with the basic necessities—schooling for their children, a house, and a car. These needs are later complemented by the luxury of taking an annual trip to see family and friends back home, sending monthly remittances to relatives in Latin America to support family members or help pay off family debt, or acquiring possessions as visible tokens of their success in life. That is why some Latinos may buy large portable radios, or spend a whole week's salary on the latest and most expensive sneakers or on heavy gold chains or medallions—all of these are evidence that the family has some discretionary income. These individuals also feel pride in knowing that during difficult times they can sell or pawn the jewelry, for example, to obtain money for the family. Better educated and more acculturated Latinos may go on cruises or dine in expensive restaurants and feel that they have made it.

Another strong motivator for work among Latinos is a sense of duty. Latinos are accustomed to complying with assignments. This motivation is closely linked to the sense of responsibility, which will be considered later in this chapter. Latinos are taught to feel ownership of the tasks they accomplish, and this sense of commitment sustains them through to the completion of a task. Still another motivator for Latinos is a strong sense of pride in accomplishment. It is important for them to know that their hard work is recognized and appreciated. A job well done reflects a person's upbringing as well as the support he or she receives from spouse and children. All of these are strong motivators to do a job well.

When goals are seen as group initiatives, their effectiveness will multiply. An example is the case of the Latino manager of a rapidly growing bank branch. The bank's proximity to a bustling commercial district brought in a large number of customers, but limited staff meant that the teller lines were endless. The tellers were as efficient as they could be, but there were times when the lines were unreasonably long. Every time the Latino manager saw this, he would come up behind the tellers and say, "*Muchachos* [a generic term for both boys and girls], let's shorten this line." Then he would take a seat in an empty teller's booth. Immediately, a rush of energy would run through the room. Thirty minutes later, the line would be back to normal and the manager would return to his office. This was not a planned strategy or a result of a performance appraisal. On the contrary, it was an on-the-spot objective set by the manager and shared collectively, giving the group a sense of oneness, of being needed to complete a task successfully.

Latinos generally need a sense of overall purpose in their lives; they need to have a goal as a reason for doing things. As an example, an employee who goes to night school is likely to be motivated by the prospect of finding a better job in the future. Following is an anecdote of the administrator of the national airport in a Latin American country. On his first day on the job, he inspected the facilities and found that the restrooms were extremely dirty. He called in the maintenance supervisor and indicated that this was unacceptable. The employee made it clear that he felt no motivation to do his job. People didn't take the trouble to clean up after themselves, he had not been given any cleaning equipment, and the previous administrator did not really care. The new boss authorized the maintenance supervisor to purchase the needed cleaning equipment and told him he had 24 hours to get the bathrooms so sparkling clean that he would be able to have a meal there—or else the supervisor would be dismissed. When the supervisor went back to his staff, now motivated by trying to keep his job, clean the bathrooms, and maintain his good name, he set them all right to work. The following day, the supervisor called the administrator to announce that he had achieved his goal. The administrator said that they would meet in the men's bathroom. He called the cafeteria and had a sandwich delivered to the bathroom. When he found that he was, in fact, able to eat it there, he told the maintenance supervisor that he had passed the test. After that, the restrooms were kept impeccably clean.

Latinos, like anyone else, need a motivation for completing their assigned tasks. If a mainstream supervisor takes the trouble to understand what motivates a Latino employee, there's a good chance to promote an outstanding job performance.

VIGNETTE

՟ Vinicio is a middle-aged event planner from South America. He came to the United States a couple of years ago looking for opportunities for professional growth. He found a job at a party facility, where his native Spanish was greatly appreciated as an asset in dealing with Latino families. Vinicio's employer sponsored his visa, and this job gave him a good chance to learn the business while also learning English. Here, Vinicio is discussing his work motivation and his frustration with Mario, a close friend and recent immigrant who is looking for a job.

> *Vinicio:* Mario, you will be able to find a good job. Be patient, and try to sell yourself for your significant differences, like your Spanish and your willingness to make sacrifices in order to do a good job. It may be appreciated by your employer.

Mario: Yes, Vinicio, I am trying. I see you got a good job and you're doing well. Now I'm hoping it's my turn. How did you do it?

Vinicio: Well, don't think things have been so pleasant for me at work, but I have found a way to survive.

Mario: Really? Why do you say that?

Vinicio: Well, I have a supervisor who screams at people when things don't go as he plans. I work with really difficult clients, who sometimes have a bad reaction because I'm Latino and can't understand their wishes. The work I do requires lots of patience—and long hours, too.

Mario: Well, I guess you had some of that back home in your previous job.

Vinicio: Sure, but at home I had more opportunity to move around. Here I'm tied to this company because of my work visa. I can't even think about looking for another job, as I would have at home.

Mario: Well, then, that does make it more difficult. How do you cope?

Vinicio: Through self-motivation. I send my parents back home money every month to pay for their food and rent. I know they depend on me. When my mom calls, she tells me how proud she is to have a son who can support her in her old age. That is worth any sacrifice. So for now, my ability to make money to meet my family responsibilities is my motivation and the purpose of my life; it is what helps me endure a less than desirable situation at work. I want to be sure my parents are doing OK, plus sending them money for their needs helps to make up for my absence.

Mario: I can imagine the happiness for your parents to be able to have peace of mind about their finances in their old age. I understand, my friend. I'll be patient while I am looking for a job, and if I'm not lucky enough to feel totally fulfilled, your situation has helped me understand that I will need to focus on my goal, which in my case is getting a graduate degree.

Cultural Pointers

- Like many Latinos, Vinicio came to the U.S. looking for better career opportunities.
- He is tied to his employer through his immigration visa, whether or not he likes his job. Because he must stay with this company, he puts up with conditions he would not have accepted at home.
- Vinicio's self-motivation is to meet his family responsibilities—a strong trait in Latino culture. His mother's satisfaction when she receives the money he sends motivates Vinicio to keep going despite his difficulties at work.
- Mario knows that obtaining a graduate degree is what is going to keep him motivated through the challenge of finding a job—and keeping it.

CONFLICT MANAGEMENT

Regardless of culture, individuals' reactions to conflict can vary depending on the nature of the event. Overall, though, Latinos tend to be good mediators because in their actions they try to protect relationships.

Latinos' initial reaction to conflict is to avoid it. Why would they want to contribute to a lack of harmony? They would prefer to wait for the conflict to go away. They may think, "If I don't recognize this situation as a conflict, then maybe it isn't." Or they may hope that, in time, some other event will take precedence over the conflict so that its importance will be minimized.

Latinos are taught not to think in terms of enemies but, rather, to look for ways of mending relationships, which is what makes them such good mediators. They generally do not express opposing viewpoints if doing so will affect their dealings with others. Confronting someone with whom they may have a conflict can lead to a situation that many Latinos find difficult to handle. As a result, they are more likely to dismiss the conflict. This may be why, when asked about their strengths in interviews, many Latinos say, "I never have problems with anyone at work" or "I get along well with others. I'm a people person." In contrast, mainstream interviewees may focus more on the effectiveness of their relationship skills in accomplishing the task at hand.

As Latinos consider an unresolved situation, they may blame themselves and try to identify whether there was anything they did to damage the relationship; in other words, they move through conflict with a sense of guilt. Because Latinos tend to be very self-conscious, they may dwell on their own perceived responsibility for the situation even if they do so only in private.

Only when a conflict reaches a critical stage will Latinos likely face it— and that is when the Latino skill at conflict resolution kicks in. As a manager, you may want to give your Latino supervisee a little push because it may take him or her longer to get to the point of recognizing that he or she needs to play an active role in doing something about it. Meanwhile, you may see him or her as acting in ways you associate with poor, subdued, passive Latino families one finds in the stereotypes described earlier.

Once they have taken the first step, however, Latinos will go into conflict resolution in a very conciliatory manner. We see this with Latino lawyers, who usually try to reconcile a separating couple before their divorce is final. In this case, the lawyer acts in the role of a marriage counselor or a religious minister, trying to identify what is needed to keep the couple together. Latinos are likely to take the same approach to relationships at work.

This trait can be a positive addition to the work environment, because, when handled wisely, the desire to establish harmonious relationships may facilitate reaching agreement. When everyone else has given up on solving a conflict, "calling in the cavalry" with Latino style may be a good strategy.

Latinos do not usually initiate friction in a work relationship, but, should it arise, they will recognize it and will be concerned. Some of their methods of resolution may be indirect, such as staying away from the person with whom there is conflict to prevent *echar más leña al fuego* ("throwing more wood into the fire"). Another tactic might be treating the person to courtesies and gifts as a sign of goodwill and to show the desire to mend the situation.

In a business environment, the desire to maintain harmony may make the Latino employee appear to be soft. More aggressive individuals may view the Latino as weak in negotiating because of the cultural tendency to express a willingness to accept the other party's ideas. In fact, because many Latinos tend to give in if they believe this will help the relationship, it may be important for managers to be very clear about how much is open to compromise.

At times, someone with this Latino behavioral style may be just what is needed to demonstrate to others what can be accomplished through a willingness to reach agreement and a desire to continue a relationship. Latinos tend to hold on to their vision of how the situation *should* be, thus appearing to be somewhat of a dreamer or naively idealistic. Whether it is because of such idealism or simply because they have been given the responsibility of negotiating, they will do their best to resolve the conflict.

If no solution seems possible, they may simply leave the situation that is causing the conflict, as is common in the case of disagreements with a supervisor; instead of confronting the issue, employees may prefer to transfer to another department or even look for another job.

Many Latinos feel that if a situation is beyond resolution, they should exit before the personal relationship is harmed. However, as long as there is hope, they will try to solve the problem. They generally want to see relationships work well, and, when they believe there is a good possibility of solving a problem, they will try to offer a win-win solution.

The challenge for Latinos, however, may be recognizing that strong personal friendships are not required, expected, or even possible in every work situation. Only acculturation to mainstream society gradually lessens this challenge.

VIGNETTE

∽ Lourdes, a second-generation Latina, and Brigitte, who is of mainstream origin, have worked together for a few months. They are both administrative assistants at a mid-sized car dealership. The differences in their styles seem to be creating conflict in the relationship. Although they sit next to each other, lately Brigitte has been quiet and distant from Lourdes. Lourdes has noticed this, and, although she has not taken any action to attempt to address the problem, at home each night she does reevaluate the day to see if she has done anything to create tension between them. Lourdes knows that something is bothering Brigitte, and she feels guilty for not being able to change that.

One morning, Brigitte approaches Lourdes right after they have both been assigned to do a task together.

> *Brigitte:* Lourdes, if we are going to be working on this project together, we need to talk. During the months since you joined the company, I have been responsive to your questions and even helped you with some tasks. However, the introduction of the new system has been intense and is trying for everyone. We're all busy while you are moving slowly through the learning process. You can't expect me to do your work as well as mine. It's really getting to me.
>
> *Lourdes:* I didn't think there was anything wrong with our work relationship. Sometimes, when I've needed your help, you've given it to me, and that's that. It should not affect our work.
>
> *Brigitte:* Sorry to disagree, Lourdes, but I think we have a problem in our relationship. I am not willing to help you with your needs at the level of intensity you require. Haven't you noticed that I haven't been the same lately?
>
> *Lourdes:* Well, yes. But I thought you must be going through a difficult personal time, which required privacy. Actually, I thought about the situation every day to see if I had created a problem for

you, but I didn't see it. And now you tell me it's because of my questions. (*Lourdes gets emotional as she continues.*) I'm sorry if I created a difficult situation for you. I did not mean to bother you with my questions.

Brigitte: Well, don't get like that, Lourdes. This is just a conversation to try to solve this situation. You know we have to work on this project together, so we must decide how to approach it to make it work.

Lourdes: OK, Brigitte. I feel I only asked questions, but if that bothered you then I accept my part in the situation and, certainly, let's consider how we can plan for this work. So, what do you propose we do?

Brigitte: Let's set aside 15 minutes every morning just to check in on how we are doing and whether there are any doubts about the project. This way we'll limit the time for questioning and get our work done the rest of the day.

Lourdes: I will also ask our supervisor to allow me to spend a few hours this week with the system's experts so I can feel more knowledgeable and not have to ask so many questions.

Brigitte: That sounds more like it.

Lourdes: Thanks. That will help me. Your friendship is important to me, and I would not like to jeopardize it over a misunderstanding.

Brigitte: Well, let's start with our work relationship!

Cultural Pointers

- Brigitte is not afraid to face conflict, especially because her intention is to solve it. Lourdes, however, tries not to acknowledge that she and Brigitte have a problem. Although she senses there is something wrong, she prefers to let time solve whatever is amiss.

- Lourdes, who is not used to this type of confrontation, gets apologetic and emotional. Her culture does not foster a face-to-face discussion of conflict. She has already felt guilty about her possible responsibility for Brigitte's attitude.

- Lourdes' goal is to re-create harmony, while Brigitte's is to try to solve a work problem.
- Lourdes is looking for closeness and friendship in the work relationship, something Brigitte does not feel comfortable offering at this point.

FORCEFULNESS

Some people, familiar with the second stereotype—the "hotheaded" Latino—discussed earlier in this chapter, may view Latinos as aggressive. In this stereotypical view, the Latino explodes emotionally, and sometimes violently, at any provocation, no matter how small. In the work environment, these might be individuals who hit their desk with their fists during a work discussion, shout at subordinates and peers, or tell the boss to "take your job and shove it."

Some Latino supervisors believe that the best way to demonstrate control is to show their authority through an aggressive style. They have been taught that being in control is what it's all about and that showing a sense of equality is a sign of weakness. Sometimes this aggressiveness is used as a sign of power and authority, minimizing the importance of others who work for and with this person.

It is true that many Latinos can be passionate about their feelings and wishes. As a rule, however, because Latinos tend to seek harmony and to avoid conflict, their style may appear to be more passive than aggressive. This lack of aggressiveness can be positive in the sense that it can create a work environment with minimal conflict, where one person rules and the rest follow. But it also has a negative aspect, because Latinos may not seem as forceful in completing a task or in making a statement as their mainstream counterparts (*Longman* 1997). The Latino is likely to say something like, "It may be appropriate to consider another way to solve this problem," or, "Others might think that . . . ," thereby placing himself or herself at a distance from the contending points of view.

Aggressive behavior in the sense of having drive and tenacity is highly valued in the U.S. work environment as a way of achieving goals and facing challenges. For example, corporations expect their salespeople to actively pursue leads. They expect employees to be tough negotiators for the company and to demonstrate their effectiveness by tackling projects with assertiveness. Latinos understand this, and the more acculturated ones will respond readily to such demands. First-generation immigrants, however, may have a tougher time.

In Latino culture, aggressive behavior can have a negative connotation; it may imply a desire to attain one's own goals at the expense of others (Sosa 1999) or to portray oneself as something one is not. Latinos may struggle with the idea of having to market products they know their clients don't need or doing a project they know will not be successful.

Individuals with high potential are sometimes characterized as aggressive. They are bright and effective but may also be high-maintenance and difficult to please. They face everything with tremendous drive and initiative. Latinos will tend to see individuals who exhibit such behaviors as never fully satisfied, always knocking on one's door asking for more. They may interpret such behaviors as signs of immaturity and greed, in terms of what such employees are willing to do to attain their goals. Many Latinos believe that progress must not be achieved at the expense of others. Therefore, if a new position is open, one that includes a promotion, a Latino who desires it will most likely just sit back and hope that the supervisor will consider him or her, without formally expressing his aspiration for the new job.

Consider the situation of a Latina employee working on a project that was about to conclude. She needed to either find another job within the organization or leave. Although she had some time to find a new assignment within the company, she was required to actively look for a job. She did have an interest in an open position in another location as project leader. Her technical expertise was unquestionable and perhaps the highest of any of the candidates. However, the supervisor was doubtful about her ability to lead. The Latina candidate in question was waiting passively for the manager to invite her to join their group. She did not show any sign of enthusiasm for the job. The hiring manager saw this as an indication of her lack of aggressiveness and leadership and wondered if this was also the way she would tackle the project. Fortunately, the employee's current manager, in a conversation with the hiring manager, realized what was happening and strongly encouraged her to formally express her desire for the new role. In this case, the employee's lack of drive and aggressiveness almost caused her to lose the opportunity for the new job.

Latinos prefer to take the necessary time to develop credibility and trust in order to accomplish transactions in a cordial way, rather than pushing ahead. In the previous case, the candidate believed that she would be the favored candidate on the basis of her work history. She did not want to appear overly ambitious by forcefully pursuing the open position. She simply did not realize that she would also be judged on the way in which she conducted the job search itself.

VIGNETTE

Harry Longlow, of Irish English background, works as a salesman for a cosmetic firm. Luis Febles, a second-generation Latino, works for a similar company. The two manufacturers have developed competing brands of lipsticks, which they hope to introduce into the market rapidly. Each salesman visits Miriam Salas, the purchasing manager for a large beauty salon franchise. Each man's presentation reflects his cultural background: One is aggressive in his sales approach and the other is not.

HARRY AND MRS. SALAS

Mrs. Miriam Salas: Hi, Mr. Longlow, come in—I was expecting you! (*They greet with a strong handshake.*)

Harry Longlow: Mrs. Salas, thank you for meeting me. I know your time is valuable, so I'll be brief.

Mrs. Salas: That's fine, you always bring me good products.

Harry: Thank you. That is my goal. Today I wanted to introduce you to this fantastic line of lipsticks. Take a look at all of its great features—low cost, long-lasting, waterproof, and it comes in 20 different colors, including the colors that appeal to teenagers.

Mrs. Salas: Sounds interesting, but they're probably more expensive than other brands.

Harry: Of course, but in order to make the deal attractive to you, I can give you a 10 percent savings as an introductory price.

Mrs. Salas: Tell me more.

Harry: Well, as an introductory offer, we can have one of our models present for the first week to help you sell the new line in your store.

Mrs. Salas: I think my clients would like that.

Harry: Great! You'll find many competing products, but don't be misguided—none with this quality.

Mrs. Salas: Yes, but the competing products are also quite good.

Harry: You'll soon see that ours are better. I have the invoice with me for your order, but of course I will certainly answer any questions you may have.

(Mrs. Salas is somewhat perplexed at having to make a quick decision and evaluates whether or not she should jump at the offer.)

LUIS AND MIRIAM SALAS

Mrs. Miriam Salas: Come in, Mr. Febles, I was expecting you.

Luis Febles: Hola, Sra. Miriam! It's a pleasure to see you again. How have you been doing?

Mrs. Salas: I'm OK. Working harder than I want to, but with the holidays coming up, everything needs to be ready.

Luis: I know, it's the same for us, but I'm sure we'll find time to spend with the kids later.

Mrs. Salas: Sure we will, after we get the stores ready for the holidays.

Luis: Talking about that, Sra. Miriam, how have your sales been? I know that beauty products have been hard hit by the recession.

Mrs. Salas: Somewhat slow these days, but I'm hopeful it will pick up soon.

Luis: I'm sure it will. Well, thank you for your courtesy in giving me a few minutes of your time. We have had a long business relationship, and our products sell well in your store, so I thought I should stop by to let you know about this new lipstick line.

Mrs. Salas: Interesting, but can you really make anything different in a lipstick?

Luis: Well, we realized many young girls pay attention to their looks earlier than before. Believe me, I know, because I have two teenage daughters at home! These new lipsticks come in colors especially designed to appeal to teenagers. They're waterproof and long-lasting to suit girls' active lives. Besides, the price per unit is very affordable.

Mrs. Salas: It sounds attractive, but how does your product compare to that of your competitor?

Luis: Well, our competitor also has good products, but you see, we've brought lots of innovation into ours.

Mrs. Salas: Well, that sounds appealing. What will prices be like?

Luis: Just a little bit more expensive, but I think you will find these new lipsticks will be worth the price. If you think you would like to try them, I can give you an introductory offer.

Mrs. Salas: That's good, because it will allow me to test the product with our clients without a large investment.

Luis: Sure, and you may want to take this opportunity to do a nice launch. We can work together to organize it. Actually, we have some models available who can offer counseling to your young clients for the first week.

Mrs. Salas: Well, then, I guess we can try a small order and see how it goes.

Cultural Pointers

- Harry and Luis are both effective salesmen, and they have a good chance of selling their products. The difference is in the way they approach the sale, based on their cultural backgrounds.
- Harry goes straight to the point, giving his sales pitch very professionally. In contrast, Luis is easygoing, and the meeting is more of a conversation. Mrs. Salas does not experience any aggressiveness in his presentation.
- Harry remains detached from Mrs. Salas, while Luis calls her by her first name (although for respect he introduces the title "Sra." or "Mrs.") and takes time for some initial small talk.
- Harry favorably compares his products to those of his competitors. In Mrs. Salas's view, this approach may make him look aggressive. Luis discusses the competition only at the request of Mrs. Salas.
- Luis shows a caring attitude toward Mrs. Salas and tries to involve her in the conversation by touching on personal issues before getting into his sales pitch. He even mentions his personal situation, having two teenage daughters at home.
- Luis, unlike Harry, is not pushy or aggressive in the closing. Whereas Harry talks about invoices, Luis mentions them only indirectly. He focuses on the relationship and the service he provides to customers rather than on the product.

SENSE OF RESPONSIBILITY

The importance of meeting obligations, taking ownership of tasks, and seeing them through to completion is generally well ingrained in Latinos. This generally results from the sense of duty that Latino parents teach their children at an early age. They are taught to take care of younger siblings because the oldest child should protect the family. They are taught to pick up their toys, because their mother works and is tired when the day is over; to get good grades, so they can be "someone" in life; and to be respectful because their elders are wiser than they. Trying to do things well is innate in Latino culture. This is not necessarily linked to effectiveness, but for Latinos the effort has as much merit as the result.

A Latino will willingly make personal sacrifices to deliver results, whether by taking work home or by coming to the office on weekends. Family members may even offer to help complete work projects at home. As much as Latinos care about balancing family and work on a daily basis, if they are required to finish a task, they will give responsibility to their job a high mark.

At times, the Latino sense of duty may push a worker to accept an inordinate amount of work and to develop multitasking capabilities. This may be a product of parental advice early in life to be cooperative and responsible. A Latino parent always says, "I will leave you my good name, take care of it," indicating that although material wealth can be lost, one should never risk the family's long reputation for hard work and integrity. Thus, Latinos carry with them responsibility for protecting the family name. Latinos are often referred to as "Maria's daughters" or "Jaime's nieces" instead of by their own names, so the person's behavior is tied to the family.

For Latinos, work comes before play. Their desire to please both family members and authority figures may lead them to take on tasks that will push them to do more work than they can reasonably handle.

You may be thinking, "But aren't Latinos generally relaxed about time and deadlines?" And this may be true. If you consider punctuality as part of being responsible, you may have a point because of the very different Latino sense of time. However, if you clarify for a Latino the reasons that you need the work completed at a specific time, it will usually get done. You have now given the Latino employee a responsibility for the solution, and he or she has been taught to live up to that responsibility.

Thus, if you tell a Latino caterer that you need the catered meal there "for lunch," he or she may think it makes no difference whether the food arrives at noon or at 2:00 P.M. The exact time will depend on his or her delivery schedule. But if you say you need the lunch delivered on Friday at noon because it's your daughter's wedding, he will go all out to get it there on time.

Latinos tend to be good at multitasking and may become proficient at performing several roles at once. In mainstream restaurants, for example, the greeter is there only to welcome you and ask you the number of guests in your party. You wait for your table, while another person comes to clean it as the previous guests leave. Still another one will come to set the table freshly for you. Only then will the waiter come to take you to your table, and he or someone else will be responsible for taking your order. You have only been in the restaurant a few minutes, and you have already seen four people working to serve you.

Latinos may feel impatient with this unfamiliar protocol of specialization. In a Latino-run restaurant, by contrast, the greeter may be the owner's daughter Margarita, who is given that position because she knows English well and is good-looking. She will greet you like family and count your party on her own. She immediately takes you to your table, while her brother Raul clears the table and lays new place settings, most likely with you already sitting. They know service is important and thus they are trying to be fast, not rude. After all, you set and pick up the table at home, so why should this be done before you come to the table? Raul needs to be quick, anyway, because he has to get back to the kitchen to help Mom and Dad prepare the meals. Margarita is left to ask hurriedly for your order so she can go back to being a greeter. This anecdote may slightly exaggerate the point about multitasking, but it is not far from examples we encounter daily. It's the contrast between the employee who says, "Its not my job to do that," versus the one who says, "Just tell me what needs to be done and I will do it; that's what I'm here for."

As noted earlier, in a desire to please employers, some Latinos may overcommit themselves. This may have a negative effect on their performance, hindering their ability to meet deadlines or affecting the quality of their work. In the previous anecdote, if Raul were only responsible for setting tables, he would probably not have to do so with the guests already seated. If Margarita only took orders, she would not be looking up constantly to see if new guests were waiting for her at the door. For employers, however, this multitasking ability is a valuable trait, because many Latino employees are likely to have the potential to perform several roles at once and to be willing to dedicate additional time to work.

VIGNETTE

৩৩ Juan is a responsible employee from Central America who has very slowly moved up the corporate ladder. Now he is at the peak of his career and is already thinking about retirement. Although Juan has been in the U.S. for some 15 years, having immigrated as an adult, he has still kept many Latino traits. Juan was recently given the task of assessing market conditions for a new strategy and has exceeded himself in terms of the hours he is putting in. His supervisor, Alex, seeing the situation, has a conversation with him.

Alex: Juan, I wanted to let you know that I am very happy with the way you are taking care of the strategy-setting project we assigned you. You seem to be doing a very good job.

Juan: I am pleased to hear that. I am trying my best to get you the results soon because I know we are very pressed for time.

Alex: I know time is short, and I feel confident you will be on time. Precisely because I can see that happening, I wanted to talk to you about the way in which you are going about the project. I have heard that your doctor recommended that you take it easy because you are very stressed, but the security officer tells me that you are only going home every night for three or four hours. And your secretary let me know that you are not even taking time for lunch.

Juan: Well the project has been difficult. You know the market is quite unpredictable these days, so setting a strategy we can live with requires a lot from me.

Alex: That's precisely the point, Juan. We appreciate you and would not like to see you become ill by doing this project. What's going on?

Juan: Well, Alex, these have been a couple of intense months. I was not feeling well, so I visited my physician. He indicated my heart was giving me some problems and I should slow down somewhat. However, I have this huge responsibility, and I need to accomplish our objective within the prescribed time frame. I'll deal with the rest later.

Alex: I admire you for your dedication and discipline, but it seems unreasonable for you to have to work this way.

Juan: This is the only way I know. I was taught to be responsible. Some little heart problem is not going to slow me down. Don't worry— I'm taking the pills the doctor ordered, and I should be fine.

Alex: I hope so, but I want you to consider taking a few days off.

Juan: That I will not be able to do. I have tight deliveries for the following month.

Alex: But, Juan, can you at least go back to a normal schedule?

Juan: You know I need to put in those extra hours or we won't be on time, and I don't feel comfortable working from home, so the best option is extending my work schedule.

Alex: How about additional resources?

Juan: That will eat up all of our budget, so I'm not sure that is a good idea.

Alex: I don't know what else to suggest to you. Why are you doing this to yourself?

Juan: Well, that's just the way it is. I was taught by my parents to be responsible and fulfill my obligations. I feel the company has placed a lot of trust in me by assigning this project to me. It's a matter of family honor. I cannot let my father down, and I must make my mother proud. Don't worry, I'll rest when we are done.

Cultural Pointers

- The mainstream supervisor is caring and shows concern for Juan.
- Juan recognizes that he should take it easy, because the physician did find some problems when he had his medical checkup.

- For Juan, however, a sense of duty is much stronger than the desire to take care of himself. There is a deadline and a task that he needs to accomplish.
- Although the manager suggests some ways to alleviate the pressure, Juan is so committed to meeting his deadline that he finds excuses not to use any of the options.

Unfortunately, the story in the vignette is a true one. The person we refer to as "Juan" did have a stroke related to the stress at work. He barely survived and had to leave the organization. He was left with speech and physical impairments. However, his sense of responsibility was inspirational to many.

RISK TAKING

Latinos are not usually associated with a high appetite for risk taking. Evidence of this is the fact that decisions tend to be shared. Sometimes the person has already made up his or her mind about the best direction to take, but will still feel a sense of duty to ask, because, in Latino culture, that is the right way to do things.

In many organizations, the Latino style is seen as conservative and prudent—as showing little appetite for risk. This can actually be a positive competency at work, because Latinos will be wary of anything that may jeopardize the final objective. However, making decisions with the least possible risk is not always the most effective approach in business, and it may jeopardize potential opportunities for success.

Latinos are more prone to taking risks with people they know well. Because theirs is a relationship culture, they begin by learning to trust others; once someone trusts them, they try to meet that person's expectations.

After a recent death in the family, my (Francia's) sister was trying to order some flowers for the funeral, which would be held in a Latin

American country. There was some inconvenience involved in accepting a credit card order over the phone (a mainstream reader should be aware that this may be the case in some Latin American countries). After several tries to find a payment method that would be acceptable to both parties, the woman in the flower shop surprised the caller by saying, "I have seen your efforts to try to find a solution to this situation. I have seen you try to make three-way calls to contact relatives in the country to be able to cover you. I will trust you. I will deliver the flowers for the funeral, if you can get someone to come in tomorrow to make the payment." The flowers were delivered and the payment was promptly made. This happened because the woman in the flower shop was willing to take a risk; she had developed a sense of trust in the caller through their telephone interactions with each other. True, Latinos are sometimes hurt, because some people may not be responsive to this behavior, but for the most part they will not let someone down who has trusted them.

VIGNETTE

෴ Luisa came to the United States from Paraguay in search of work opportunities. She has been in the U.S. for only three months. Her move involved taking substantial risks. Luisa shares with Margaret, a mainstream friend, what immigration has meant to her.

Luisa: Margaret, I have to admit I'm not a big risk taker. I don't even play the lottery! Very few things have caused me to make drastic changes in my life, and even fewer that were initiated by me.

Margaret: We're taught somewhat differently in the U.S. We learn to take risks, because people move around to different states, switch jobs, and take on new and challenging tasks.

Luisa: Yes, that's what I've seen. However, I don't think a Latino would do that as easily. I am always fearful my actions may harm the people I love or that I might expose myself to risk. I usually prefer not to take such risks, even if it means missing out on a good opportunity.

Margaret: Sure, Luisa, and I've heard Latinos are very conservative, however, you did move to the U.S. very recently. I would certainly say that is an example of risk taking. It sounds like a big decision, especially if you are not inclined to take risks. What made this one worth taking?

Luisa: It was perhaps the biggest risk I will ever take, but I had a goal, and after careful assessment and lots of family involvement, we all felt it was worth it. After all, the worst that can happen is that I may have to go back home. I'm here to begin to secure a future for the family members I left behind, so the risk is worth taking.

Margaret: Except for that summer I spent in Paraguay, I have never lived outside the U.S. So what is it like, moving permanently to another country?

Luisa: It is like pulling out a plant by the roots. You leave your country, family, friends, job, and practically everything you have built for yourself. You come to a place you don't know, where the language and the people are new to you. You have nothing to hold on to, you have no support group.

Margaret: Well in my eyes, Luisa, you are a risk taker. I'm really impressed!

Cultural Pointers

- Although Latinos are not big risk takers, they are capable of managing great risks. Such is the case of Luisa and her decision to immigrate.
- Immigrants face challenges and obstacles because the immigration process involves taking huge risks. Willingness to go through this process is, in itself, evidence of an individual's courage to explore the unknown after assessing potential gains.
- Luisa took time to make her decision. She consulted with people she considered knowledgeable and evaluated her options carefully. Before

taking action, she assessed her risks and decided it was worth the gamble because of the goal of securing a future for her family.

RESOURCEFULNESS

Latinos tend to be recognized for their high degree of resourcefulness. They are able to find ways to handle situations that may be considered difficult to manage.

This is likely the result of their experience learning to survive and deal with a myriad of difficult scenarios in their countries of origin. For example, some Latin American countries have serious energy and water shortages; people may have to endure long lines at gas stations because of fuel shortages; and they may even lack basic foods, such as sugar or rice, for extended periods. These hardships affect even those who may have the money to buy these things, because the shortages are a result of the country's level of development.

This resourcefulness became apparent to me (Francia) when, after I moved to the United States with my family, my son's school announced that there would be a trip to the Everglades. I asked him the purpose of the trip, and, as my 11-year-old interpreted it, the idea was that the students would learn about nature and see what it was like to be in a different environment, which he translated as one with mosquitoes and without electricity, running water, or restrooms. We always laugh at the memory of this experience. We decided to view it as an opportunity for my son to get to know his new classmates. But based on the way he saw the experience, my natural response would have been to tell him, "Son, you have just arrived from a Latin American country. Back home you experienced all of that. What you need now are lights, highways, and fast-food restaurants. *That* should show you a different environment."

Living in a less-developed country prepares people for difficult situations, so when Latinos arrive in the United States as immigrants, they have already learned to be creative in meeting their family's needs and have become very resilient. These two traits—resourcefulness and resiliency—serve Latinos well in the work environment here. They have developed a tough enough skin to cope with difficult bosses, survive disappointing work situations, and stay focused on the goal of making it in the demanding environment of the United States. That is why, as noted earlier, a Latino worker is likely to show persistence, flexibility, and drive in attaining established work goals.

Latinos have also learned to deal with challenging situations. I (Francia) clearly recall the summer that my non-Spanish-speaking American nephew came to visit us. I took him with my own kids for ice cream, and, as we were heading home, university students involved in a protest demonstration were headed down the main street where I was driving. I could see that there were also policemen ahead of me, so I expected there could be trouble. I began planning an escape route, and I told the children, "There's danger—take cover." My kids instinctively lay down on the floor of the car—not because they had received any special war training but simply because they had been "taught" how to react during a period of social unrest. Meanwhile, my gringo nephew was sitting up straight, totally perplexed as to what my words meant and what to do next. Latinos may, in general, be better prepared to recognize danger and, rapidly and resourcefully, find a way to deal with it. The fact is that in our original home environment we have sometimes had a wide range of experiences that we can use to our benefit. We may be better equipped than mainstream individuals to cope with the unexpected, the uncertain, and the bizarre, as well as with life's many inconveniences, because many of us come from countries where assault or kidnapping is frequent, where we have experienced guerrillas or civil unrest or even drastic political and economic measures.

A Latino thus may also be quite experienced in figuring out how to overcome bureaucratic red tape by pursuing innovative ways of obtaining services or accomplishing tasks in a challenging environment. Latinos who show this ability in the U.S. workplace should be quite successful in creative thinking—"thinking outside the box" (Muller 1997). At times, some Latinos may mistakenly believe they can solve problems in the U.S.

in the same manner that they addressed them in their countries of origin. As they go through the process of acculturation, they learn—sometimes the hard way—that the U.S. is a different environment.

VIGNETTE

☙ This hypothetical situation involves Rosaura Ramírez and Al Stevens, employee and manager of a bed-and-breakfast in West Palm Beach. Al had moved from Seattle looking for a warmer climate. He was born into a middle-class family who were able to provide for his basic needs and to send him to a community college, where he took some courses on the hospitality industry. He had been exposed to few Latinos before coming to Florida.

Rosaura comes from the Dominican Republic. She had learned English in after-school classes, and her family was poorer than Al's. She finished high school at night in her home country and worked as a maid during the day before moving to the U.S. five years ago. She is a documented immigrant.

According to the bed-and-breakfast's hurricane plan, all guests had to be evacuated and the hotel prepared for potential strong winds and flooding. During the heavy 2004 hurricane season, when several of these giant storms headed for Florida, West Palm Beach seemed to be right in their path. Al had just flown to Seattle when he heard the advisory of the hurricane, so Rosaura was left on her own. Fortunately, her resourcefulness as a result of having experienced hurricanes in her country proved to be even more beneficial than Al's hurricane plan.

As soon as communication was functioning, Al phoned to see how Rosaura had handled everything.

Al: Rosaura, it was a good thing we had a hurricane plan. This one hit hard. How did you deal with everything?

Rosaura: The plan surely helped to get organized, Al, but there were many things I improvised on as I went along, which were not part of the plan. You are lucky I have lived in a country that has hurricanes and other strenuous situations and I know what to do.

Al: What do you mean?

Rosaura: Well, for starters, not all guests were able to leave. The shelters were full, so they had to stay in the hotel.

Al: Really? We never intended for that to happen. How did you handle it?

Rosaura: I decided to put them all in the safest room in the house—the kitchen. This way we had food, water, and restrooms nearby. We made out OK. I had them play cards during the hurricane to keep them entertained.

Al: That was a great risk, but I'm glad everyone is safe. I know we had an excess of refrigerated food, so that shouldn't have been a problem.

Rosaura: Oh, food we had, but without electricity the fridge was not of much use after a few hours, so I separated the perishable food from that which could last longer. I gave everyone steak for breakfast and didn't charge them for meals. It was going to go to waste anyway.

Al: I'm glad to hear that, Rosaura. What other things did you have to cover outside the plan?

Rosaura: Well, the lack of electricity was certainly a constraint for washing the towels, the bed sheets, and the guest clothing. So a couple of hours before the hurricane I had everyone deliver to us what they needed washed and dried for a couple of days. This way everything was washed, dried, and ironed before it hit.

Al: That was clever. How did the building sustain the hurricane? Did you get hold of the people who generally put up the shutters for us?

Rosaura: The building was more or less OK. We were not able to get the guys who put up the shutters because everyone was busy. So a couple of my cousins came to help and under my direction they put up the shutters. They knew I had a big responsibility, so they supported me and did a fine job.

Al: Anything else?

Rosaura: Well, I have many other things to comment on, but I guess I'll wait for your return.

Al: Thanks for everything, Rosaura. I'll be there soon and we can revisit my hurricane plan. It seems you know of many more things it should include.

Cultural Pointers

- Al is used to having things done in a structured and planned way. His work style involves having contingency plans to face strenuous situations. He trusts things will work as he has calculated.
- Rosaura is aware of the contingency plans, but she is prepared to anticipate and face the unexpected. This is how she got by in her home country.
- Rosaura thought of innovative ways to support the bed-and-breakfast in the midst of the coming hurricane in a way that Al had not anticipated. This included managing how to keep the unexpected guests safe and cared for in the hotel, dealing with electricity shortages, making use of the refrigerated food, and even having all the linens and clothing in the hotel washed and dried before the storm hit. It also included Rosaura's family members pitching in to help her put up the shutters.
- Rosaura's determination, resourcefulness, and resilience saved the day.

PROBLEM SOLVING

Latinos are generally very conscious that, to get along in this world, they will need to be able to work with many different types of people. Therefore, they place a high priority on solving problems collaboratively and on thinking about how their decision will affect them personally and as a group (Morrison, Conaway, and Borden 1994).

Latinos may be uneasy with the mainstream culture's transactional, fact-oriented approach to problem solving. Although they can see the effectiveness of this method, they may feel that solving problems in this way proceeds much too quickly and places feelings at a distance. They are likely to be more comfortable with an experiential approach to resolving issues. This includes looking back at their experiences for the right answers, as well as consulting with others.

Latinos may be perceived as individuals who resolve problems at a slower pace because they take the time to evaluate how their actions will affect others. Thus, they may give the impression that they are distracted and not moving along in the intended direction, when in fact efforts are being made behind the scenes. This slow, deliberate approach creates a kind of security blanket to ensure that interactions are being handled in an adequate manner and that effective steps are being taken along the way.

This difference in approach is seen in the way mainstream and Latino individuals, respectively, tend to close a business deal, as exemplified in the following vignette.

VIGNETTE

֍ Pedro Paniagua and James Scott are successful partners in a small medical equipment company. They have been trying to penetrate the Latino market and are discussing an equipment problem of one of their clients, Dr. Gómez, who proved to be a difficult account to get. Pedro, who is of Latino background, and James, of mainstream origin, have equivalent skills and business know-how, but they have very different views on how to approach the situation.

> *Pedro:* James, I just had a call from Dr. Gómez, our client on the Mexican border. He is having some trouble with the ultrasound equipment we sold him a couple of months ago. I promised to discuss the situation with you and get back to him.
>
> *James:* Why would you need me to help you solve his problem? Why didn't you just go ahead and send the technician? All Dr. Gomez wants is for the equipment to work properly.

Pedro: Sorry, partner, but this time you are mistaken. Dr. Gómez is a Latino. Although we have been successful in selling him the ultrasound equipment, if all we do is service this malfunctioning machine, we may lose his account.

James: I don't get it. Why would the account be at risk if we are doing what he wants, which is making the equipment work properly?

Pedro: Because the relationship here is more valuable than either the account or the equipment.

James: What do you mean?

Pedro: Well, it's similar to when we discussed the selling strategy for Latin America. Your proposal at the time was to get an appointment through the secretary, offer our products through our brochures, and close with a telephone order. But you'll remember, that didn't work until I got an appointment with Dr. Gómez with the help of my aunt, who is a patient and dear friend of his. Once I got to meet with him, we discussed how we had met before at my aunt's birthday party. I remembered that his son was studying medicine and recognized him for his support for the community.

James: I remember it took a while for us to get the account, and the process seemed somewhat burdensome to me.

Pedro: Yes, but we succeeded by explaining the advantages of being able to service the patients visiting his new clinic and of understanding his needs over a period of time. Nothing happened until a sense of trust was developed and the relationship was strengthened.

James: So how do you propose we handle this now? I don't want to lose the client, but I'd hate to spend a lot of time and effort again on the same account.

Pedro: I suggest that I go with the technician who is going to solve the problem. This will show Dr. Gómez that we care about him and his needs, that we're not just making a piece of equipment operable. I don't have to stay more than a day, but he will see our commitment and care.

James: Well, Pedro, if this is what you think will retain that client, go ahead. I'll take care of things here at work.

Cultural Pointers

- James's approach is based on solving the problem and doing so in a short amount of time. This is his interpretation of what the client wants. In this case, he is approaching a Latino client as if the client were mainstream—that is, seeing a problem and solving it mechanically.
- Pedro uses a Latino approach, trying to solve the situation through relationship building. He knows that solving the equipment problem will not be enough and that trust could be jeopardized. His way will take longer and might cost more, but it will probably prove his commitment, and, as a result, they will likely retain the client for a long time.
- Dr. Gómez will see that—aside from the company's care in making the ultrasound equipment operable—they also want him to feel comfortable with the relationship and trust that they will be there when he calls.

ETHICS

Although, as noted at the beginning of the chapter, one stereotypical view of Latinos is that they are unethical, take advantage of others, and live on the wrong side of the law, such cases are the exception rather than the rule.

The large majority of Latinos work well in environments that demand integrity, compliance, and accountability. They greatly value doing the right thing, largely because of their strong religious base that establishes this behavioral norm for most Latinos.

Latin America is, however, well known for public officials and politicians who take bribes; it is thought of as a place where everything can be bought. For example, some people agree to pay for services that are supposed to be provided for free and pay higher prices for other services in order to expedite them. At times, the dilemma is that some of the same people who take bribes or are individuals on the wrong side of the law are also generous to their own communities. One hears stories of drug lords who are greatly appreciated in their birthplaces because they have used proceeds from their illegal dealings to finance schools, hospitals, and housing projects for the community. Their sense of community and giving back to others may not take into account how that money was obtained. There is a sense of ethics that accommodates to the needs of the group, where they all seem to share a common objective. This is also the case of political appointees who collect bribes for their services so that they can share with relatives. They justify this practice because they are paid miserably for their jobs.

At times, the way the system in Latin America works may lead some to believe that a little bit of wrongdoing is okay, especially if the purpose is grander than the means. People may even joke that "white sins" (lacking severity), much like "white lies," will not keep you out of Heaven. Therefore, the level of the possible moral penalties depends on the severity of the wrongdoing. This attitude makes it difficult for Latino parents to teach their own children the right way to behave. For example, whereas teenagers in the U.S. will read the driver's manual and then go and take the driver's test, Latino teenagers may instead try to find a friend of a friend who can help them get their licenses without taking the test. It can be hard for parents to persuade their children that in the U.S., facilitating transactions through a network of bribes is not an acceptable way to do business. This may be seen by the Latino as facilitating a service and not as an illegal activity. Most likely, though, the Latino's sense of religion and family values will win out, and he or she will question and judge wrongdoing.

VIGNETTE

☞ Federico Ramírez, a new security officer, is being interviewed for a job with a multinational company. Although he has had previous experiences with global firms in Latin America, he only recently transferred to the U.S. Marianela Portoreal, the staffing manager, needs to verify his position on ethical issues before his hiring can be confirmed.

Marianela Portoreal: Mr. Ramírez, please tell me about a situation where your ethics were tested.

Federico Ramírez: Well, while I was working back home, some employees were wrongly using company cars. It was not a major offense, just weekend trips here and there. I could have looked away because they were my friends and good workmates, but I preferred to solve the situation, at whatever cost I had to pay.

Marinela: And how did you do that?

Federico: Well, I sent out a memo with new guidelines and requested that all cars be left on our premises over the weekend. I was not the most popular person after that, but the misuse of the company's assets was corrected. This was the best way to do it, because it prevented me from having to tell on my colleagues.

Marianela: Why did you feel you had to do this?

Federico: My family is recognized for our honesty. My father always had positions where he could have done the wrong thing. However, he kept the family name clean. I am the oldest son, and I need to continue that tradition.

Marianela: That speaks highly of your family values. How do you personally feel about dishonest people?

Federico: Well, we have to live with all types of individuals, and some of them may not be honest. But when I see that something unethical is happening, I have to act. I was always taught to take a stand in these situations. It doesn't matter what price I have to pay.

Marianela: Sure, but that makes you unpopular, and I'm sure that sometimes you are rejected by others for your strictness.

Federico: Then that is something I will have to live with. I can't change my values and principles.

Marianela: Certainly that puts you in confrontation with other people, and many Latinos do not like that.

Federico: Of course we don't, but you see, we put our ethics ahead of our personal preferences. Sure, we don't like to have bad relationships with other people, but doing the right thing comes before anything else.

Marianela: What does "doing the right thing" mean to you?

Federico: For me, doing the right thing means taking my responsibility seriously, making sure I do what is expected of me. I don't mean only at my job. A job can go away, but I still need to live with the person inside me. My principle is that every morning when I look at myself in the mirror, I need to be able to keep my chin high for the sake of two people— myself and God.

Marianela: That is a great attitude, Mr. Ramírez, but it implies more work for you and it also may create enemies.

Federico: As long as I am doing what is right, I have no problem with having fewer friends. The way I see it, if these people don't have good work ethics, maybe they should not be in the company, anyway. And I certainly don't want them as my friends.

Marianela: Well, that is an excellent answer, and we are very glad to consider you as candidate for our security position. We'll let you know our results shortly.

Cultural Pointers

- Federico is ethical for several reasons: He has been taught to do the right thing and is loyal to his employer, but above all he values protecting the family name.

- Federico is willing to pay the price for doing the right thing even if this makes him unpopular or means confronting someone who is not behaving in an ethical manner.

- Federico's sense of ethics is high. Marianela feels comfortable in terms of his work ethics.

- Although Marianela may have wondered why Federico didn't directly reprimand the individuals taking the company cars, being of Latino origin, she understands that in Latin America most of the time what he did is enough and that the practice was eliminated.

We have seen in this chapter how day-to-day practices may be handled differently by a Latino and a mainstream individual. Latinos' motivation to work, their sense of responsibility, and their work ethics are highly linked with religiosity and family image. Their resilience, apparent low appetite for risk, and problem-solving methods may even be interpreted by the mainstream as weak, time-consuming, unfocused, and unstructured, despite the fact that these may be effective approaches from the Latino perspective. As a manager, peer, or subordinate of Latinos, it is advisable to assess the reactions and behavior they may exhibit before jumping to conclusions. They may just have a different way of approaching a situation, and the approach is likely to lead to similar results.

CHAPTER SEVEN

Contrasting Aspects of Latino and Mainstream Cultures

Harvey Stone has an M.B.A. from a prestigious university on the East Coast, where he graduated with honors. He interviews for a mid-level managerial position at a bank branch. When asked why he is interested in the position, he lists three reasons: First, he wants the job so he can apply his experience and skills. Second, he would like to use the new challenges as a vehicle for developing more senior-level managerial skills. Finally, he adds, he has been in his current job for more than two years and he feels it is time to move on. Harvey also mentions that friends who work for this bank have shared with him that the benefits package is very attractive.

Rosa Perez, a competing candidate for the position, is a second-generation Latina whose parents emigrated from Central America in the 1980s. She has an M.B.A. and graduated first in her class seven years ago. Here is how she responds to the same question. First, she wants the job because she is committed to honoring her father, who worked as a janitor for the same bank for 20 years. She would be honored to be able to work for the same bank that helped her father send his children to college. Second, Rosa explains that she is interested in advancing her professional development and eventually becoming branch manager in order to have the opportunity to use her cultural skills to manage and mentor a large emerging Latino workforce at the branch. She hopes to mentor others in order to give them the opportunities she has had.

If you were the interviewer, how would you evaluate Rosa's and Harvey's responses? Rosa's responses reflect loyalty to the bank that employed her father, pride in her cultural heritage, a need to honor her family, and a passionate desire to succeed. Harvey's responses indicate that he is ambitious, competent, and concerned about his career progression, which are the expected responses in the mainstream culture. His focus is on his individual goals and on professional progress, not on staying at the same job very long. However, his responses do not reflect other qualities that would likely emerge with additional probing.

This example highlights the focus of this chapter—that some values of the Latino culture affect the way Latinos perceive and express ambition, loyalty, leadership, pride, honor, and success. In this chapter, we will describe these concepts and highlight both the contrasts and the commonalities that seem to exist across mainstream and Latino cultures with the purpose of providing insight into their practical applications in the work environment.

Table 7.1 summarizes the cultural perceptions of Latinos and mainstream individuals regarding the meaning of these six cultural aspects.

AMBITION

In both Latino and mainstream culture, *ambition* is one's drive to achieve goals. Cultural differences exist, however, in what drives ambition. Many mainstream individuals tend to focus on obtaining wealth and power. Often, the reward is gaining visibility and public recognition. In contrast, for Latinos, ambition is a force that pushes them toward obtaining desired social, educational, and financial goals. The reward is having the ability to improve their family's life.

Latino Interpretation   Ambition may encompass a very wide range of aspirations, depending on an individual's educational level, generation,

Table 7.1. Contrasting Views Regarding Some Latino and Mainstream Culture Perceptions

Concept	Latino Culture	Mainstream Culture
Ambition	Drive to achieve goals leading to the well-being of family members	Drive to attain personal wealth, power, and recognition
Loyalty	Fidelity toward family, friends, group, and employer	Allegiance to employer who meets the employee's expectations
Leadership	Recognition given to those in positions of authority	Quality ascribed to those who have demonstrated an ability to guide others
Pride	Associated with country of origin, family, and overcoming challenges in order to give family a better life	Associated with personal accomplishments
Honor	Distinction based on public recognition of commendable performance, pristine reputation of family	Recognition bestowed on those who show exemplary behavior or achievement
Success	Recognition that has a positive impact on the family	Achievement of desired personal goals

and social status. In describing his parents' business ambition, Hector Barreto, appointed as the head of the Small Business Administration in 2002, referred to it as a desire to accomplish a great goal, a quest, a combination of vision and drive (Radelat 2002).

For many Latinos, ambition is the drive that can help the family enjoy life together. For example, owning a house instead of living in a rental property is seen as conducive to attaining well-being for all family members. It is probably for this reason that many Latinos use their earnings to buy homes. Joel Kotkin and Thomas Tseng have reported that over 50 percent of Latino net worth is found in home ownership, in contrast to 32 percent for the total U.S. population (2002). Latinos have a great deal of respect for families who own their own homes because it indicates that their income qualifies them for a mortgage loan.

The spiritual or sentimental aspects of life, such as the family, are more important than material wealth in Latino culture. Latinos often talk about the importance of "being" rather than "doing" or "having"—of enjoying each moment to the fullest. A Latina may say, "My husband is honest and hard-working. It doesn't matter if we don't have luxuries as long as there is food on the table and my children are healthy." This non-materialistic perspective suggests that ambition is an aspiration to give value to one's life by providing for the security and comfort of the family rather than by focusing on attaining material possessions or achieving significant financial success.

Many Latinos view those who have a great deal of ambition as individuals whose disproportionate greed may lead them to believe that the end justifies the means. Among Latinos, it is often said that a person who is too ambitious at work may be willing to climb on others' backs without any regard for hurting people, simply in order to reach the top. A person who is perceived in this way may encounter difficulties in gaining the trust of Latino peers in the workplace, because they tend to avoid close relationships with such individuals. Take the case of a young Latino graduate of an Ivy League university in the U.S. who was somewhat of an outcast among his peers after he returned home to work in a Latin American company. In his computer, he kept a list of those workmates who had graduated abroad and tried to strengthen ties with only those individuals.

Mainstream Interpretation In the mainstream culture, personal ambition is what drives an individual to attain goals such as wealth, power, or recognition, and it is focused on accomplishments. Regardless of an individual's level of education, the mainstream culture values individuals whose drive has led them to own and have control over extensive assets, to demonstrate unique abilities, or to perform unusual feats. For many mainstream individuals, being ambitious represents the road to success. At times, marriage and family become a lower priority.

Application to Workplace There are important implications for the workplace in the differing definitions of ambition between Latinos and mainstream individuals. In the mainstream culture, individuals are expected to exhibit ambition when they are applying for a job. When a promotion is on the horizon, many mainstream individuals are willing to make personal and family sacrifices in order to present the image of an employee who is on his or her way up the career ladder.

Although some extremely ambitious Latinos may be willing to sacrifice personal and family life to attain their personal goals, most Latinos accept greater responsibilities at work only if a promotion can help attain family-centered goals such as buying a car, qualifying for a home mortgage, or paying for children's college education. Sometimes, once these goals are attained, the prospect of having more time for the family may be more attractive than a promotion.

VIGNETTE

֍֎ Esther Prada, a second-generation Latina and VP for human resources development, meets with John Evans, the company's CEO, to discuss a concern that is likely to affect her area's annual strategic plan.

> *John Evans:* Hi, Esther, have a seat. What's on your mind?
>
> *Esther Prada:* We're out of compliance with the federal government, John. We need to increase the percentage of minority middle managers this year.
>
> *John:* Don't we have several minority people working as entry-level managers in the pipeline? I imagine they would jump at the opportunity for a promotion.
>
> *Esther:* Well, we do have two Latinos with graduate-level degrees who are due for one.
>
> *John:* So, what's the problem?
>
> *Esther:* They don't want more responsibility at work; both of them just got married.

John: Doesn't an increase in compensation make the idea of a promotion appealing?

Esther: You would think so. But I've spoken to both, and they're not interested.

John: Isn't there a way we can entice them?

Esther: Well, a perk that would definitely entice them would be if the company could help each couple buy a new house.

John: Is that what it takes? Then pursue it, by all means!

Cultural Pointers

- Esther must have the CEO's support in order to increase the diversity of managers in the organization and be in compliance with federal law.
- As a second-generation Latina, Esther is familiar with and understands her parents' culture, and she uses this knowledge to better understand her Latino staff. She knows what's important to them.
- Esther knows that John's perspective is very clear-cut. She negotiates with him to make the promotion more appealing to the two candidates she has in the pipeline.

LOYALTY

In both mainstream and Latino cultures, the concept of loyalty evokes an image of allegiance and fidelity. But whereas mainstream individuals may take a more rational and individualistic approach to being loyal, Latinos are more emotional and collectivist, often even passionate, about loyalty. In addition, the rationale that leads individuals to maintain or suspend loyalty may differ in the two cultures.

Latino Interpretation The Latino view of loyalty encompasses attachment or devotion that tends to be more collectivist than individualist (Salgado de Snyder 1987). The attachment often includes a strong emotional component and may involve dedication to country, family, or religious icons. For example, a Latina may use a brand of detergent, regardless of its quality, because her mother used the same brand. An employee who is somewhat dissatisfied with the service provided by a company will nevertheless maintain the business relationship because a family member works for that company.

When Latinos take loyalty to the personal level, they mean fidelity toward a dear one such as a spouse or a close friend. They express this fidelity in very emotional terms, whether an objective rationale exists or not. For example, an employee may support a cousin's stance at work even if not completely convinced it is the right thing to do, because expressing solidarity with a relative—that is, family loyalty—is more important than showing objectivity.

A number of cultural values may color loyalty. Latinos are loyal when they perceive respect, *simpatía*, and *personalismo*. Aware of the buying power of this group, many companies are dedicating considerable efforts to capture Latino loyalty. For example, respectful bank officers gain Latino customer loyalty with personalismo—by knowing the clients' names and showing simpatía toward family issues (Heaney 1986). Some organizations gain the loyalty of employees by using familism and respect for Latino cultural values. For example, companies that invite family members to their holiday celebrations have higher retention rates for Latino employees (Todd 2001).

Mainstream Interpretation In the mainstream culture, loyalty may be contingent on being satisfied; therefore, it often involves a rational process. For some, loyalty involves adhering to the norm. Thus, mainstream individuals remain loyal to companies that provide services and products to them as long as these products are rendered as expected. In the corporate world, loyal employees are those who show dedication and allegiance to the organization. They are considered trustworthy because of their loyalty. However, even a loyal mainstream employee who is unhappy with compensation and benefits may explore opportunities with the competition.

Application to the Workplace As we have said in earlier chapters, Latinos are usually very loyal to their employers. They tend to stay with an organization even during difficult financial times, especially when their hard work is acknowledged. Loyalty to a company is enhanced when Latinos perceive that their jobs are stable and that there is a caring environment at work. They value supervisors who display personalismo and simpatía. When managers establish effective, caring, one-on-one communication, Latino employees will be productive and will express their appreciation by sharing positive opinions about their employers with relatives and friends in their communities. In sum, the emotional expression of loyalty is evidenced in the way Latinos behave as employees.

When the Latino is a supervisor, loyalty toward the organization is generally very passionate. He or she will work long hours and handle company issues as if they were personal matters. Latino supervisors may, as we mentioned earlier in this book, adopt a paternalistic attitude toward employees. Although this is a cultural trait, it is also a way of ensuring that employees maintain a satisfactory relationship with the organization.

VIGNETTE

൭൭ María Escobar has worked as an administrative assistant at the headquarters of a large law firm for five years. She is one of 10 administrative assistants, many of whom joined the organization when Christine, the head administrative assistant and office manager, let them know about open positions. María, who is one of the youngest administrative assistants and has been with the organization for only one year, recently received a bachelor's degree from the local state university, which she attended at night. She is surprised when she hears that one of the partners, Mr. Jones, has asked to see her in his office.

Mr. Jones: María, please come in. I am very impressed with your annual performance review. You're rated as an exemplary employee.

María: Thank you.

Mr. Jones: I met with our human resources director last week, and, based on this review and on the fact that you have successfully completed your degree, I've recommended you for the position of office manager.

María : But what about Christine? She's the office manager. And she's great at managing us.

Mr. Jones: I believe you have the skills necessary for this position. And I would like to transition you into it.

María : Please don't get me wrong. I appreciate it, but I can't accept Christine's position.

Mr. Jones: It's my responsibility to make sure we have the right people in place so that we can attain the firm's goals. You're the best candidate for the promotion.

María : I can't betray Christine. What will the others think of me?

Mr. Jones: Maybe I should have started out by saying that you'll have a substantial salary increase.

María: I'm sorry, Mr. Jones. It's not about salary. I cannot do this to Christine. She taught me a lot when I joined the company. She's my friend.

Cultural Pointers

- Mr. Jones is convinced that María has better skills for the office manager position than Christine. He is offering María a promotion and an increase in compensation. María isn't aware that Christine's performance has lagged during the past year.

- María believes that accepting the position would amount to betraying Christine. For María, loyalty to her group, and especially to Christine, is more important than getting a promotion.

- Although the dialogue does not reveal this, María also has a hard time imagining herself supervising her peers, especially because most of them have been with the organization for longer than she has. Also, three of her colleagues are older than she is, and she feels she owes them respect because of their age.

LEADERSHIP

In the mainstream culture, individuals must earn recognition as leaders. In contrast, as you now know, many Latinos tend to grant respect automatically to individuals in positions of power. They also view such individuals as leaders by virtue of their status. In a study of televised drinking and driving warnings conducted with Mexican American and Anglo young adults, Anglo participants rated warnings that did not feature the surgeon general as more believable, whereas Mexican Americans found the warnings with the surgeon general as the more credible source. In their eyes, the person with power was the leader, the one they should believe (Perea and Slater 1999).

Latino Interpretation For many first-generation Latinos, a leader is generally someone in a position of hierarchical, political, or religious authority. For example, Latinos will refer to the Pope as the leader of the Catholic Church, to a President as the leader of the country, and so on.

Perhaps reflecting the evolving generational composition of this population, an article published in *Latino Leaders* magazine recently defined leadership without including status in the definition, rather "as a human virtue, social phenomenon, and a life achievement." The author further discussed the concept with a combination of the collectivist Latino perspective and the individualist mainstream view.

> Individual leadership emerges everywhere, leadership to accomplish our own personal successes, but collective and social leadership is harder to find. It involves helping a whole community, a city, a nation, the world get on the road to success. When a leader

starts making his or her community successful, it guarantees not only personal success, but also a place in history and in the hearts of many people (Ferraez and Ferraez 2004).

Mainstream Interpretation In the mainstream culture, leadership is a status ascribed to those whose personal qualities make them appear worthy of guiding others. The recognition of a person as a leader is often an acknowledgment of the individual's vision and outstanding personal qualities. Managers who aspire to be true leaders are expected to possess both administrative and human resources skills. Given that many work environments are multicultural, managers with sensitivity, cultural awareness, and knowledge of acculturation issues are the most likely to be seen as having leadership qualities (Warner 2000).

Application to the Workplace The concept of *power distance* plays an important role in Latinos' relationship with managers. For example, Latinos may prefer a paternalistic boss; they may be more satisfied with a directive and persuasive manager and will try not to disagree with him or her (Warner 2002). This suggests that they perceive their supervisors as leaders. They respect them and do not feel the need to question their instructions. Latinos, as we've learned, tend to treat their managers with politeness and respect, agreeing to follow instructions even when a task seems unreasonable or impossible to accomplish (Deforest 1994).

A mainstream supervisor who wishes to establish an effective and productive relationship with Latino supervisees should be aware of this behavior. The best approach is to exhibit simpatía and encourage Latino employees to ask questions, while acknowledging their respect for you as their leader. On the other hand, a Latino supervisor may perceive a lack of respect on the part of mainstream direct reports who ask questions. A sensible approach would be for mainstream subordinates to express respect verbally before asking questions.

Latino employees look up to a manager who, in addition to having authority, also acts as a Latino leader would. Thus, they enjoy working for supervisors and managers who respect their cultural values and who lead by example. On the other hand, Latino managers' leadership skills are often enhanced by their work ethics and personalismo in their interactions.

VIGNETTE

૭૭ Robert Smith, CEO of a pharmaceutical company, makes an unannounced visit to Carlos López, director of product marketing. Mr. Smith is the founder of the company and interacts with most of his senior employees on a first-name basis. Carlos, who has been with the company for five years, is a second-generation Latino with an M.B.A. in marketing.

Mr. Smith: Hi, Carlos. How's your dad? I remember he used to work for me. (*He offers a handshake.*)

Carlos López: Hi, Mr. Smith. My dad's fine, thank you. He always remembers how you grew this company from 20 employees to more than 1,000.

Mr. Smith: Be sure to say hello to him for me. Now, on to business. For years I've encouraged research to develop new drugs for diabetes and hypertension. That's where the big bucks are, and that's also how we'll be able to help a lot of people. I'm a diabetic myself.

Carlos: I didn't know that.

Mr. Smith: We're getting ready to launch two new products, one for diabetes and the other one for hypertension. I believe it's important to focus on the Latino market.

Carlos: That makes sense; diabetes and hypertension are very widespread health problems among Latinos.

Mr. Smith: Right. Our success with Latinos will serve as a platform to market our drugs to other groups. I want you to lead the team that will be working on this project. Your expertise and knowledge of the culture will be critical in helping us market them.

Carlos: I appreciate your trust in me.

Mr. Smith: With the growing Latino population, we should capture a good share of the market, since our prices are very competitive. And we will also help improve the health of Latinos.

Carlos: Absolutely!

Cultural Pointers

- Mr. Smith's visionary leadership helps him recognize Carlos's talent and cultural heritage. He decides to designate Carlos as the leader of the team in charge of marketing the two products because Carlos can relate to the prospects they want to reach.
- Carlos looks up to Mr. Smith as a person of authority and is honored by his decision. Although it isn't directly stated here, Carlos also feels that Mr. Smith has an aura of credibility and is a leader with vision.
- Familiar with the Latino culture, Mr. Smith establishes a flow of simpatía and personalismo between himself and Carlos during the conversation.
- Carlos's heritage emerges as a personal motivation. He sees the opportunity to help improve Latino health and is proud to lead the team.

PRIDE

Pride is a state of satisfaction that individuals exhibit based on who they are, who they identify with, or whether they have achieved their goals. The mainstream culture rewards an individualistic notion of pride, contrasting sharply with the collectivist Latino stance, which focuses on the family.

Latino Interpretation For Latinos, pride is a profound feeling often associated with familism and collectivism. It is common to hear Latinos express pride in their families by saying, "We're proud to be members of the Martínez family. People respect us because they know we're honest people." Most are proud of the results of their efforts in working hard to raise a family, buy a house, and give their children the opportunity for a college education. They take pride in knowing that their children are good citizens and productive members of society. They also take collective pride in their country of origin. Many Latinos, too, pride themselves on having successfully overcome the challenges and hardships related to their immigration to the United States.

Mainstream Interpretation On an individual level, mainstream individuals express pride as a high degree of self-respect and satisfaction because of their exceptional personal skills or outstanding professional accomplishments. When mainstream individuals feel pride, they may also consider the endless personal opportunities that lie ahead.

Applications to the Workplace Latinos pride themselves on their contributions to the workplace, especially with regard to an outstanding work ethic. Supervisors who place a great deal of importance on the work ethic will seldom be disappointed by Latino employees, who value the opportunity to put their skills to work for a company. Sharing aspects of their culture that may help solve work-related challenges, when appropriate, is another source of pride for Latinos. In a multicultural environment, providing such opportunities to all employees can lead an organization to create a workplace where all employees feel they and their culture are valued. In particular, first-generation Latinos are often eager—and proud— to share aspects of their cultural heritage with coworkers, if given the opportunity. They feel a strong sense of pride in who they are and what they have accomplished—for example, having legalized their immigration status and having a job.

Immigrant Latino supervisors and managers who have worked for organizations in their countries of origin, where resources were often limited, may feel pride in the wealth of experience they have to share and in the ways in which they can be an important asset to their organizations—increasing productivity, controlling costs, and decreasing unnecessary expenditures.

VIGNETTE

෴ Michelle Post works at a large department store where she supervises a team of 20 sales representatives who have won the most awards in the store during the last five years. Michelle has received only one bad report from the customer service department about a sales representative, Gloria Molina. Michelle, who prides herself on being objective, immediately meets with Gloria to investigate the situation.

Michelle Post: Thank you for coming to meet with me. Have a seat. Gloria, I have to tell you that two customers complained about your attitude last week. Do you remember either of these situations?

Gloria Molina: I do. It was last Wednesday.

Michelle: Do you know why the customers complained?

Gloria: Yes, I had a couple of calls from home while I was waiting on both customers. I had to take the calls, and the customers got upset because they had to wait. But this is the first time a customer has complained about me. You know, I take pride in my work and especially my service to customers.

Michelle: I know that. Would you like to tell me more?

Gloria: Not really. All I can say is that it won't happen again.

Michelle: You have been an exemplary employee up to now, Gloria. As a matter of fact, I recommended you for a salary increase a month ago. I'd like to help.

Gloria: Well . . . (*she hesitates*) the calls were from my husband. He was at the doctor's office with our son. He needed information about my son's allergy history and medications. My son is a straight-A student in school, but his asthma is a big problem. My husband and I are taking turns caring for him. I haven't missed even one day of work in the last five years.

Michelle: Well, I was hoping there was a good explanation for your distraction. I understand now. But if you get an important personal

call again, I suggest that you ask a workmate to cover for you while
you take it.

Gloria: I will.

Michelle: I'll report the outcome of our meeting to customer service
right away.

Gloria: Thank you for being understanding. You won't need to speak
to me again about this.

Cultural Pointers

- Michelle is proud of her team and of the way she supervises them,
  with objectivity and a caring attitude.
- Gloria is very proud of her performance at work. She was embarrassed
  about the two incidents with customers. However, nothing is more
  important to her than her family. Gloria did not want to explain the situation to her supervisor; she feared that Michelle would not understand.
- Michelle persisted because she knew that if she showed simpatía and
  sensitivity, she would probably be able to help Gloria.

HONOR

Honor is as important to Latinos as it is to mainstream individuals. However, the definitions of honor may differ in the two cultures. As with so
many other Latino traits, honor is a family matter. For many mainstream
Americans, the focus is mostly on individual recognition.

Latino Interpretation When a Latino excels at work and receives a commendation based on performance, family members also feel honored.
Many Latinos associate honor with the family's social standing. They are
extremely protective of the image of their family members because the
credibility and reputation of any of its members represent the family's
honor.

Honesty and integrity bring honor to the family; the lack of either one will damage the family's honor. For example, some people may avoid interacting with a certain family because one of its members had a legal problem. In the Latino community, where social networks and collectivism are so important, the family's honor is a priceless asset. Shameful family situations such as bankruptcy, a lawsuit, a child who fails a grade at school, or an abusive husband are kept very private. Public knowledge of these issues can undermine the respect that others may have for the family and tarnish the family's honor.

Gender issues associated with honor are very important. Young Latinas are raised to be very modest in their relationships with males. For unmarried women, suspicion of prenuptial intimate contact, loss of virginity, or pregnancy can be very damaging to the family's honor. This attitude is more evident in traditional Latino families. Wives are supposed to be virtuous, modest, and conservative in the way they behave and dress in order to maintain the decorum expected of all female family members. In many Latino families, children, regardless of gender, do not leave the parents' home until they marry.

Mainstream Interpretation In the mainstream culture, honor is high respect or esteem bestowed on individuals whose actions and behavior reflect an exemplary code of excellence, integrity, or valor. This recognition is highly valued because it fosters credibility and respect and often opens the door to new personal opportunities. For example, a soldier who receives a medal of honor often becomes a model and mentor for peers; a student who graduates with honors will often expect to obtain future academic distinctions and work opportunities.

Application to the Workplace In the workplace, Latinos strive to maintain high performance standards and a strong work ethic. When employers show satisfaction with their work, Latino employees are pleased that they have been able to demonstrate that they are good workers. The recognition of their performance brings honor to the family. They feel especially honored when their performance can influence mainstream employers to recruit other family members.

Latinos feel honored when they receive public praise, recognition, or a letter of commendation from a supervisor. Although the honor is bestowed on the individual in the work environment, the impact is greater at home, where family members can express their joy in knowing that one of them has been acknowledged.

VIGNETTE

෨෩ Stephen López owns a landscape company. He receives a report that one of his employees, Roberto Castro, an immigrant from Mexico, may have broken an expensive piece of his equipment. He calls Roberto to his office.

Mr. Stephen López: Roberto, I believe you had a problem with the big lawn mower yesterday.

Roberto Castro: Yes, Mr. López, but it's working fine now.

Mr. López: Can you tell me what happened?

Roberto: The lady offered to pay me on the side if I did additional work that was not included in the work order. I told her that I would do it but would not take her money, and that I would let you know that I had done the extra work. Then the lawn mower overworked and malfunctioned.

Mr. López: How come it's working now?

Roberto: I took it home last night. My brothers and I fixed it.

Mr. López: I'm relieved to hear it. I've always thought very highly of your family. When your two uncles worked for me, they were among my best employees. I was hoping you had a good explanation.

Cultural Pointers

➤ Mr. López shows respect toward Roberto during their conversation. He also mentions that he has known Roberto's family for years. Some of them have worked for Mr. Lopez in the past. By showing respect for Roberto's family, Mr. Lopez acknowledges that Roberto comes from an honorable family.

- If his boss had not asked, Roberto would not have mentioned the incident because he did not want to complain about the client's request. He is happy with his job and trusts his boss. He feels that it was his duty to fix the lawn mower in order to protect his family's honor as well as his employer, who trusts him.
- Roberto's family worked together to fix the problem: The Castro family honor was at stake.

SUCCESS

As with all of the aspects discussed in this chapter, mainstream Americans measure success with an individualist yardstick, whereas for Latinos success is a family affair. For Latinos, most achievements bring the greatest sense of success when they affect the family, even though, from a mainstream perspective, they may appear to be personal accomplishments. For example, a Latino who is a recent college graduate will perceive himself successful to the extent that his family members acknowledge their pride in his achievement. His accomplishment translates into respect toward his family from other Latino families with whom his family has a relationship.

LATINO INTERPRETATION

Many Latinos consider themselves successful when they have attained goals that can lead to providing a better life for the family. For example, getting a college degree can lead to buying a new house, getting a new car, or helping a sibling get a college education. Attaining success is not the purpose of Latinos' lives; it represents *a means to an end*.

Latinos hold various views of success, depending in part on their country of origin and on personal circumstances. For Central American immigrant students, success means having overcome poverty, social displacement, and prejudice (Moncada-Davidson 1996). With Mexicans' growing rates of higher educational attainment, they have become more competitive in the labor market. For them, becoming upwardly mobile in their companies may be synonymous with being successful.

For less acculturated individuals, success may be defined in terms of having overcome cultural barriers, reflected in perceived acceptance, respect, and friendly attitudes from coworkers. Those who are still going through the process of acculturation may define success as being able to learn to adjust to the mainstream culture or to speak English. Others may consider finding a job as being a success. In addition, women appear to be contributing elements to the redefinition of success as, in increasing numbers, they become successful small business owners (Sarason and Koberg 1994).

Many highly acculturated Latinos' definition of success may be similar to that of the mainstream culture. According to *Hispanic Business* magazine, the typical member of the magazine's "influentials" is a male, 40 to 60 years old, who has attained a graduate degree and whose annual compensation is over $100,000 (2003). Others incorporate a Latino cultural ingredient. *Reader's Digest,* in their Spanish edition, recently published an article about the Jiménez sisters, two Latinas who have achieved high honors at Harvard. In describing their success, the sisters alluded to the way in which their parents taught them to be proud of who they are and of their origins. They believe it is possible to achieve academic success and also have a family (Fisher 2003). Thus, they appear to define success as attaining a balance between professional and personal life.

Mainstream Interpretation In the mainstream culture, success means the achievement of a desired goal. Successful individuals stand out, excel, perform better than most, overcome challenges, and are competitive (Althen 2003). Achievements must be measurable and visible and often can be translated into material terms (Stewart and Bennett 1991). Many consider financial status, power, or recognition to be measures of their success. For mainstream individuals, having a corner office or holding a high position in the organizational structure is a sign of success.

Application to the Workplace It is useful to get to know Latino employees' country of origin and whether they are first-, second-, or third-generation immigrants. This may make it easier to understand their priorities and their perspective on success. For example, for those who view success as the ability to buy a house, the prospect of an increase in compensation may stimulate increased productivity. For others, success may mean getting a college degree. In that case, offering a flexible work schedule may help to recruit and retain Latino employees. For many older Latinos, success means being able to see their children graduate from college. For many Latinos of Mexican origin, buying in the U.S. or building a second home in their town of origin, close to their relatives' homes in Mexico, provides the greatest sense of having achieved success in the United States. It can be a great source of respect from other family members. For many Latinos, success represents God's reward for being hardworking, honest, and a good person.

VIGNETTE

⊙⊙ José Rodríguez immigrated to the United States 43 years ago. He married María Salazar, a Mexican immigrant woman from his hometown, two years after he became a farmer in California's San Joaquín Valley. Eventually, Mr. Rodríguez bought land and, with his four sons, started a family farming business. His three sons attended college, and all six of his grandchildren currently attend undergraduate or graduate school. As a founding member of the local chamber of commerce, Mr. Rodríguez prides himself on saying that his family's business reputation is impeccable. In this vignette, he goes to the bank to meet with Mr. González, his banker, who is also of Mexican background but is mainstream and college-educated.

Mr. González: Hi, Mr. Rodríguez. How's the farm?

Mr. Rodríguez: Well, we had a great harvest this year. In fact, I'm here to make the last payment on the tractor loan. Finally, all of our equipment is truly ours.

Mr. González: Congratulations. If you're planning to expand your business, you may want to consider a loan. Our interest rates just went down.

Mr. Rodríguez: Actually, my wife and I have been talking about retiring. I am 63 years old. My son Roberto is taking over the management next month. From now on, he will make all of the family decisions. You may want to ask him—he may be interested in buying more land to expand our operations.

Mr. González: So what are your plans?

Mr. Rodríguez: This summer, when my wife and I go to Mexico to visit our relatives, we'll buy a nice piece of land and we'll build a house there. It's a goal we've been working toward for many years. Now, it's finally going to happen.

Mr. González: Congratulations. I'll call your son Roberto, as you suggest.

Cultural Pointers

- Mr. Rodríguez is a successful businessman by U.S. standards. By Mexican standards, he has also achieved success by providing for his family and supporting his sons through college.
- Mr. Rodríguez's idea of success includes building a second home in Mexico. Owning property there will give him and his wife recognition from extended family members and friends.
- His son Roberto Rodríguez will now enjoy the recognition given to him by his father. He will take care of the business and the family.

THE IMPACT OF CULTURAL VALUES

A *cultural script* is a communication pattern shared by members of a specific cultural group. This pattern consists of the values of the group and the behaviors that characterize it. For example, simpatía is a cultural script that links Latino respect and dignity with behaviors that seek har-

Table 7.2. Latino Cultural Values Associated with the Concepts of Ambition, Loyalty, Leadership, Pride, Honor, and Success

Concept	Associated Cultural Values
Ambition	Familism, collectivism, respect
Loyalty	Familism, personalismo, simpatía, collectivism, respect
Leadership	Religion, personalismo, simpatía, power distance, collectivism
Pride	Familism, collectivism
Honor	Familism, collectivism, respeto, gender issues
Success	Familism, respeto

mony and avoid confrontation (Triandis et al. 1984). Along these same lines, Latino behaviors related to ambition, loyalty, leadership, pride, honor, and success may be expressions of cultural scripts linked to Latino cultural values. Table 7.2 suggests some of these values.

In this chapter, we presented some important aspects of Latino culture that may have a strong impact on cross-cultural communication in the workplace. We contrasted Latino views with those of the mainstream culture to highlight the importance these differences may have in interactions among employees and with supervisors and managers. In Chapter 8 we will explore the traditional roles of Latinos as supervisors, employees, and colleagues. The concepts we have presented in this chapter, as well as the values we have explored in earlier ones, play important parts in how Latinos perceive these roles.

Latinos as Supervisors, Employees, and Colleagues

A Latino father talks to his son as he drives him to the son's first job. "Son, this is an important moment in your life, and we are all proud of you. I am going to give you my five golden rules of work. Use them wisely, and you will progress and be productive in your career." Here they are:

1. Always be grateful to God, to family, to your community, and to your employer.
2. Your supervisor is a person to trust. He will be there for you when you need him. And when you become a manager, manage with care, but be tough with those who do not respect basic values and principles.
3. Work hard and well. Be respectful and courteous. Make us proud of you and don't forget what we've taught you.
4. Show respect for authority, and never hurt others, but don't let anyone offend our name. Be true to your values.
5. Don't be overly ambitious, and you will get what you deserve.

These rules exemplify many of the Latino values we will examine in this chapter, as we explore the traditional roles of Latinos as supervisors, employees, and colleagues. We have either touched on or explored most of these values in earlier chapters, but here we will discuss these values in more depth and also focus on personal distance and professional style among Latinos. By *personal distance* we refer to the sense of closeness exhibited by a Latino in a work relationship. By *professional style* we mean behavioral style (authoritative versus paternalistic) at work. Latinos generally have a clear idea of what is expected of them in a working role. Their ideas are affected by culture, but they are also influenced by experience, upbringing, and personality.

LATINOS AS SUPERVISORS

Every important moment in the life of a Latino, whether it's an engagement, a baptism, or a graduation, implies family involvement, and there are generally *many* family members to include. A professional promotion to a supervisory role is no different. Such an event will be an occasion for phone calls to inform relatives of the person's professional progress. There may even be family celebrations to share the accomplishment in the relative's career. Those living in the U.S., far from their home countries, may call relatives in Latin America to have a conversation that begins, "My brother, I am calling you to let you know that my son got promoted to manager in his job. As head of the family, please make sure that the rest of our relatives are informed. You have been an example to my boy, and I wanted to give you that satisfaction. . . ."

In many Latino families, getting a promotion or any form of work recognition may naturally result in a celebration dinner with parents, grandparents, and children. Getting the first job and, after that, any promotion implies sharing. Therefore, the person is taught to share part of that first salary with others to maintain his or her good fortune. Envelopes with money, even if the amounts are small, are likely to be delivered to parents, grandparents, and aunts and uncles. A contribution to the church is also usually expected, because sharing with strangers is a way of thanking God for one's good fortune. Advancement at work is an opportunity to celebrate, but also to learn about giving.

In many Latin American countries, companies announce promotions to management or inclusion in a new company by placing a notice of the event in the local newspapers. This serves as a way for the company to express their appreciation of the employee's development while simultaneously serving as a form of public recognition for the individual. Some U.S. companies also facilitate the publication of names of their new associates in local newspapers, especially in businesses where the link to the community is crucial.

When a Latino is promoted to a management position, family members not only celebrate the promotion but also share a collective feeling of triumph, because all members of the nuclear group feel they have contributed to this success. A Latino will likely indicate that this accomplishment would not have been possible without the support of the family, and this is most likely an accurate statement. Close-knit family ties give the individual the freedom to be able to fulfill his or her professional responsibilities. This is the case of the grandmother who supervises the grandchildren's upbringing while the mother travels overseas for business reasons, or of the stay-at-home mom who keeps the house running while her husband works hard at his job. This is not to say that other cultures do not recognize family members in their career progress, but for Latinos this recognition has the status of an obligation.

In mainstream culture, reaching a supervisory position is perceived primarily as an individual accomplishment, the consequence of the person's professional effort. The support the individual may have had from family or mentors is not necessarily highlighted. A mainstream man is not likely to indicate that he owes his promotion to his dad, who paid for his education, and to his mom, who baby-sits while he and his wife go out to work. For a Latino, however, such acknowledgments are customary. Family support may go beyond household logistics and extend into the professional arena. To this day, my (Francia's) mother reads the newspaper every day from front to back, for the sole purpose of cutting out articles on my sister's and my selected careers, as her personal contribution to keeping us up-to-date.

A Latino or Latina supervisor will often display a paternalistic or maternal approach (see Chapter 5 for explanations of these terms), which is more intrinsic to the culture than gender specific.

Obligations for a Latino supervisor generally include being a mentor, a role model, a coach, a financial supporter, and a friend. It is an unwritten part of the job description, something we naturally fall into, and a role that may become as important as the job itself. For a Latino, being a supervisor implies having an attitude that most of us consistently maintain in our personal relationships, that of "providing care for loved ones" (Mendoza 2002). The image that Latino supervisors project at work can be equated to the one they have with their families. It implies exerting power with a caring attitude, delivering results responsibly, and providing support for those who depend on them.

Twenty years ago, when I (Francia) started my career, my supervisor also took care of my public image. He was careful not to send me on business trips outside the city accompanied by a male colleague. I either traveled alone, if he felt it was safe enough, or a companion was assigned to accompany us. This was my supervisor's social response to protecting me as a Latina. He was aware that otherwise there might be negative judgment of my behavior, and he certainly did not want to be responsible for that. In those days, one heard of supervisors who asked the husband's permission to have a female subordinate participate in events celebrated in a hotel. In closed and highly structured Latino societies, meetings in hotels could imply opportunities for inappropriate encounters. Today, it is customary for females to travel alone and to participate in whatever setting their work may take them to, but some Latino supervisors, especially those of the older generations, may still have similar thoughts as they decide whether or not to assign a task to their Latina employee.

Latinas who attain supervisory or executive positions may, as noted in Chapter 5, need to invest more effort than their male counterparts to establish recognition of their position with other Latino employees, the result of machismo regarding females in the work environment.

During a professional seminar, I (Francia) encountered a group of Chilean colleagues who, after three days of training, took the opportunity over dinner to ask me and the only other woman in the group why our husbands let us work and travel alone. Latino males may have different points of view; whereas my husband had no problem with my work or participation in overseas events, others would never have allowed their wives to travel the way I do. Along the same lines, if I had been designated as the supervisor of these same Latino males, I would certainly have had a tough time gaining their respect and establishing my position.

Personal Distance A Latino subordinate considers his or her supervisor to be the closest person of authority capable of providing support when it is needed, as the person who can make decisions and solve problems, including those of a financial nature.

A Latina who worked as my (Francia's) administrative assistant once told me that she needed my help in organizing her personal finances. I had already noticed how almost every month she needed my authorization for an advance against her salary, so her request was personal but, in a sense, work related. We found some time to review her income, debts, and other expenses, and I gave her some ideas for sorting it all out. To this day, she proudly recalls how I helped her become financially conscientious. I was very glad to support her, and neither of us perceived it as an intrusion into her private life.

Whereas the Latino manager may be comfortable playing this role, a mainstream individual is likely to be puzzled by the close relationship between Latino supervisors and their subordinates. Mainstream managers may feel uncomfortable with the Latino expectation of strengthening the professional relationship by sharing private matters. This does not mean that mainstream supervisors are not considerate, but it is unlikely that they will immerse themselves in the financial affairs, or other private matters, of their employees, even if asked.

It still amazes me (Francia) how mainstream companies offer a variety of toll-free numbers for all sorts of personal matters—suicidal feelings, problems with parents who live with the employees, drugs, financial difficulties, health questions, and so on. On one level, allowing experts to take care of these issues is prudent, but it also places a distance between the employee and the supervisor. Furthermore, a Latino employee would probably not talk about these topics to an anonymous voice on the phone; in the Latino environment, the disclosure and most likely the resolution of these challenges is in the hands of the supervisor.

Consider the case of a Latina lawyer who, after a suicide attempt, came to see the firm's human resources director every time she had an urge to take her own life. The director was not her supervisor, but she was a person of authority. This director, with no specialized knowledge of how to solve the problem, nevertheless lent a welcoming ear and communicated with the woman's relatives to help her get the professional care she needed. The important issue is that the employee felt that this person in a position of authority at work could help, and that the HR director was not surprised when the Latina came to see her.

Professional Style Some Latino supervisors manage by power and fear; others may seem excessively lax in confronting behaviors that warrant correction (Sosa 1999). This results from the way authoritative and paternalistic attitudes combine among Latinos (Warner 2002). Both styles may be present in Latino supervisors, but which management style predominates depends on the individuals. They may use the styles separately, depending on the circumstances, or at the same time in a particular conversation. Therefore, it is not uncommon for an employee to leave a feedback session with a Latino supervisor with a sense of confusion, saying, "I'm not clear if he said my performance was good, bad, or something in between." A mainstream employee would have an even harder time figuring out the direction of the feedback. This all results from the Latino supervisor's desire not to hurt feelings but to maintain a congenial relationship, combined with an authoritative style.

During my (Francia's) career, I have seen many Latino supervisors struggle with dismissals, transfers, and performance feedback. The problem is that they feel their role is to *protect*, and those actions are not necessarily conducive to executing a difficult task. It is not uncommon for dismissals to be ambiguous with a Latino manager, who may even hope to maintain a good relationship with the employee who is being fired.

In contrast, perhaps because they tend to have similar educational levels, relationships between mainstream managers and subordinates tend to be more horizontal or peer-related. In a professional mainstream discussion, even between individuals at different levels in the organization, there tends to be a sense of equality because each participant is a subject-matter expert. Although the supervisor may use his or her power to make the final decision, the subordinate's expertise will likely be taken into consideration. In the mainstream culture, conversations are generally limited to professional topics and are based on work-related know-how. There is not necessarily an interest on either side in establishing a personal relationship, so, except for brief, superficial personal comments, all of the conversation relates to work.

Relationships between Latino subordinates and supervisors, by contrast, appear to be generally vertical and directive. The Latino manager can be prone to giving orders rather than discussing options and gathering opinions from employees. This may be due in part to the generally lower academic attainment and experience of the employees as compared to the supervisors. Latinos might describe the supervisor's role as that of a facilitator, whereas for mainstream individuals, the role is more that of a collaborator.

Latino supervisors may be more inclined to engage in closer oversight and allow less independent thinking. They are generally willing to delegate responsibilities to employees, especially because it is important to one's status to distribute work to others. However, Latino managers often retain ownership of decision making as a way of holding on to their authority (Kras 1995; Morrison et al. 1994).

Latinos generally do not delegate power, so there are fewer opportunities for subordinates to develop management experience. Thus, at a professional level in a Latino environment, there may be a noticeable lack of successors for vital positions. Latinos are not likely to jeopardize their own positions by allowing an ambitious subordinate to push from below. This attitude has been evident as well in some Latino political parties, where the dominant figure passes away without having selected someone to take over. As much as Latino political leaders would like to be judged well by history, they may also prefer to allow no one close by to dim their performance.

One of the highest points in my (Francia's) career was knowing that after I left my first job to pursue a graduate degree, my position was filled by *two* external hires. I felt a sense of accomplishment, as this recognized my workload capacity and the quality of my delivery. Today, having learned the mainstream way of doing things, I realize that it also spoke to my lack of planning for a successor, which probably caused disruption in the company when I left. This, however, does not take away from the fact that I practically did two jobs without feeling any sense of abuse.

A sense of duty toward employees and friends may at times influence the Latino supervisor in decisions regarding personnel actions. Obligations to the community are a priority. In this sense, collectivism, as explained in Chapter 3, plays a vital role. This is exemplified by the practice of introducing, hiring, or promoting individuals referred by friends or acquaintances. It may also mean not dismissing an employee because he or she is the son or daughter of an influential person in the community, because one knows the family, or because the employee badly needs the job. Courtesy hires are common among Latinos. This does not necessarily mean that supervisors do not use the appropriate criteria to select the best person for the job or that they don't recognize when someone's contribution has deteriorated, but it does indicate that factors outside work will play a role in work-related decisions. The most important aspect of this is that those looking for an employment opportunity expect such behavior from anyone in a supervisory role.

Consider the case of a father who headed a chamber of commerce in a Latin American country. His networks were extensive and he was well known, so when he called on his daughter's behalf to express his interest in her working with my organization, I (Francia) was quick to make an appointment to interview her. The daughter was a graduate of a U.S. university, but she came to the interview with her father. I was surprised to see him there, but as a Latina I thought that it was sweet of him to accompany her to introduce us. (In a mainstream environment, however, the interview would have been over before it began!) When I invited the daughter to the interview room, her father accompanied us, and only then did I smell trouble. He sat with us through the brief interview and even helped her answer my questions. The girl was not hired, largely because of her own lack of qualifications, but the father's attitude also played a part because of what it told the interviewer about her. The point here is that, in a Latino environment, the young woman might have been hired, and the parent would not likely have seen anything wrong with his behavior.

This sense of community and overprotectiveness can make some Latino managers appear to be shortsighted in making management decisions. This is not a sign of incompetence; rather, it is a way of balancing professional proficiency with the personal. Although these elements may seem strange to mainstream supervisors, most of the decisions prove to be good ones. It is just a different way of getting to the same place.

I (Francia) recall discussing performance and salary increases with a Latino supervisor who wanted to include issues such as marriage or the birth of a child among the factors in his decision making about a raise for a direct report. These two issues were embedded in the decision-making process and were considered as important as factors such as effectiveness and quality of performance. The Latino supervisor felt a sense of duty to provide for this special event in the employee's life. Although this approach is guided to some extent by feelings over logic, it is not necessarily a sign of managerial incompetence in a Latino environment. With personal considerations being part of the hiring process, the employee's moral debt to the supervisor and the organization is usually guaranteed.

VIGNETTE

⚭ Arturo Molina and Mario Serrano are co-owners/managers of a hardware store. Both are of Latino background. Arturo came to the U.S. three years ago, with work experience in a similar business in his home country. Mario immigrated at a young age and is somewhat more familiar with mainstream culture than Arturo is. Mario established the business five years ago, and, while living in Panama, Arturo was Mario's client. When Arturo decided to immigrate, he and Mario partnered with the intention of expanding in Latin America.

Laura, a single Latina woman, has worked in the store for a year, but her performance has not met expectations. The following vignette highlights the approach each manager might use to dismiss Laura. Arturo takes a paternalistic approach, while Mario is authoritative.

ARTURO AND LAURA

Arturo Molina: Laura, how are you doing? I have not seen your children for a while. They must be pretty grown up by now.

Laura: Yes, they are. At seven and eight, they take up a lot of my time. I hope your family is also doing well. I met your wife at the holiday party and enjoyed talking with her. Give her my regards.

Arturo: Thanks, I will. Well, Laura, I've been meaning to have a conversation with you for some time. I know we have had previous discussions regarding your job performance. For many months I have supported you, and the human resources department has coached you. You have made some progress, and for that I need to congratulate you. But unfortunately, despite your efforts, you are not performing at full speed. You are not doing well. Management has decided we cannot continue this way.

Laura: I am trying my best, but I do not get the mechanics of the position. I have to deal with a very complicated paint mixer, and I just make a lot of mistakes. I know I will eventually learn.

Arturo: I know, Laura, but management cannot wait for that, so we must come to a parting of the ways.

Laura: Are you firing me? Oh, please don't! Give me another chance, because now, especially, I don't know what I would do without a job. I have serious financial problems. You know I am a single mother.

Arturo: Well, Laura, we will not let you go without support. We will give you your severance, and I have included an additional month's pay to help you get through. I will be available if you want to use me as a reference, and if you have any problems that you think I can help you with, let me know. We will consider you if we have an opening in another area in the future, because I appreciate your effort and will always be willing to give you another chance.

As Laura breaks into tears, Arturo comforts her.

MARIO AND LAURA

Mario Serrano: Laura, as a follow-up on your performance evaluation, I have decided to dismiss you. You are aware that after our last feedback session, you were placed on probation and received coaching from our human resources department. Unfortunately, nothing has changed.

Laura: Mr. Mario, I am trying my best, but I am having trouble learning the operation of the complicated paint mixer. I just make a lot of mistakes. I know I will eventually learn. Please give me another chance, because I don't know what I will do without a job. I have a serious financial problem. You know I am a single mother.

Mario: Laura, my decision is final. Pack your things and leave immediately. The head of our human resources will explain your severance and medical insurance.

As Laura breaks into tears, Mario leaves the office.

Cultural Pointers

- Mario is focused, authoritative, straight to the point, and unemotional with Laura.
- Arturo's attempt to ease the emotional reaction takes him through a longer path, which is more typical of Latino behavior. He initiates the session with small talk about family to set a cordial tone before arriving at the inevitable.

- Arturo adopts a paternalistic attitude by explaining that he has supported Laura to make things work. As a good protector, he has given her the chance to prove herself. He talks about his feelings, indicating how sorry he is to have to let her go.

- Arturo is indirect when he communicates the decision to dismiss Laura, indicating that it was a management decision, as if he were not a part of it, and referring to the dismissal as a parting of the ways. When Laura gets emotional, Arturo comforts her, despite the fact that he is the person causing the pain.

- Mario clearly distances himself by indicating that the human resources director will deal with the details of the dismissal. He does not leave room to continue the relationship but rather closes it permanently.

- Arturo goes beyond the legal requirements in an attempt to ease the financial burden caused by the dismissal. He offers himself as a reference, even though Laura's performance has been unsatisfactory. He even suggests the possibility of future employment opportunities in the company.

- Arturo and Mario attain the same goal by using very different approaches, one paternalistic and the other authoritative. Depending on the circumstances, the same person may exhibit both styles. For example, a paternalistic person dismissing someone for an unethical behavior may react with an authoritative style. This is a response to the nature of the offense, because in the case of unethical behavior, trust and credibility are compromised.

- Laura's feelings at the end of the two dismissal meetings are quite different. If asked, Laura would likely say that Mario dismissed her as if she were a piece of trash and did not care for her as a human being. She would probably say that Arturo was kind and helped her get through the ordeal.

LATINOS AS EMPLOYEES

Latinos do not usually question figures of authority; doing so would signify a lack of respect and would be hard to deal with because it would imply breaking a bond in the relationship. Supervisors fall into the authority category because they have knowledge, experience, or power. Employees may feel that their role is to obey and to help accomplish the supervisor's goals, however unfounded they may be.

Mainstream individuals, on the other hand, are taught to question, regardless of the position of the person. One can expect mainstream employees to ask questions about any professional aspect of a job. They might ask about the nature of the job to be done, about the effectiveness of the new strategy, or about why they are not getting a larger bonus this year. With many Latino employees, however, these questions would remain unasked and thus unanswered. Latinos are taught by their culture to find the answers along the way. There is no sense of urgency to know everything beforehand. The project or task in itself is seen as the learning process that, with time, will provide the answers. Sometimes Latinos will trust God to show them the right direction, as when they say, "*Con el tiempo, Dios dirá*"—"With time, God will say."

Latino employees will also, as we've stated several times, place a great deal of value on finding balance between work and family. They tend to focus equally on meeting the expectations of their supervisors and those of their families. A Latino or Latina employee with a strong sense of duty to the family may need more time to attend to personal needs than would a mainstream individual. In Latin America, it is not unusual to hear an employee ask permission to leave work to pick up someone at the airport, take an elderly aunt to the doctor, or run an errand for the family. When Latinos immigrate to the United States and see how people provide for these family needs in the U.S., they adapt, but they may feel that they are not fulfilling what they, as Latinos, interpret as their family duties. In other words, the Latino employee in the U.S. will probably not go to the airport to meet that relative, but he will still be concerned because he didn't.

Younger generations of Latinos seem more willing to give up some family time for their careers. However, they may be emotionally unsatisfied if they do not have that balance. It is innate to their cultural upbringing. For a mainstream person, a sense of balance is also important, but in addition to family, it also includes personal activities, such as going to the gym, taking a class, or working on a hobby. This is certainly a more individualistic society.

Personal Distance A Latino will make efforts to establish a close relationship with his or her supervisor. Generally there is no intention to breach personal or professional boundaries. Nor do Latino employees see this as a quid pro quo offered in exchange for personal gain. If a feeling of closeness does not develop, the employee may interpret this as meaning that the employer does not care or that he or she is doing something wrong. Latino employees see their purpose as pleasing and supporting their supervisor. Where a mainstream individual will think of the personal goal, the Latino is more likely to think of the goal of the supervisor or the company.

For Latinos, this closeness may result in the two families meeting, participating jointly in social events, and having their children spend time together. Sometimes, the ties between spouses become stronger than that of the employee and the supervisor. Therefore, a mainstream supervisor should not be surprised if he and his family are invited to the employee's home, however humble it may be, or if, out of the blue, an employee comes to the office with a casserole of his or her mother's specialty.

Work relationships may grow so strong that they lead to a desire to establish a permanent tie. A Latino employee may ask the supervisor to become godfather or godmother of his or her child, or vice versa, establishing the relationship of *compadrazgo* or *comadrazgo*. This relationship implies continued involvement in the child's life and a permanent tie with the children's parents. Sometimes the supervisors are the ones initiating this relationship. After working together for a couple of years, my (Francia's) supervisor asked me to be his *comadre*. For me, this was an honor and a great responsibility. I was totally flattered. At the same time, I interpreted it as a form of feedback, because I judged that he must have been happy with my work if he felt that I could be a good role model for his child. Among Catholic Latinos, this godparent relationship is considered as a sacred tie, because the commitment is formalized by the Church. Thus, the new *comadre* (comother) or *compadre* (cofather) commits to fulfilling the parental role if the parent is unable to do so.

Latino employees also tend to be overly sensitive to public criticism, humiliation, and embarrassment (Deforest 1994). They have been taught to be honest, productive, and hardworking. A negative appraisal is a sign that they are not meeting expectations, and they will struggle with the criticism and may judge themselves as incompetent. When results are good, recognition is expected; if results are negative, then at least they hope for a discreet attitude. The concept of job loss through such events as corporate downsizing is rather new in Latin America. After all, how can a job just go away? In the mind of a Latino, job loss is related to poor performance, and there is no way that a Latina can explain that although she is good at her job, it has disappeared. This leads to public embarrassment.

If a Latino receives a public reprimand, he may react by making an on-the-spot decision intended to protect his image, such as quitting or confronting a manager. Pride, family honor, maintaining one's own self-worth, or "face"—these are intrinsic and deeply ingrained Latino values. Saving face often takes precedence over the consequences of a resignation. The importance of saving face may be the product of Latin America's close-knit and smaller societies, where everyone knows everyone else—and knows what everyone else is doing.

Professional Style Latino employees tend to approach issues cautiously, especially with supervisors. They generally recognize the supervisor's authority and do not want to give the impression that they are imposing their opinions. For example, instead of introducing an idea with "I was thinking," "I'm convinced that," or "I'm sure if we do this . . . ," the Latino may say to the supervisor, "You may want to consider," "There could be other points of view," "What if someone . . . ?" That is, Latino employees are more subtle, diplomatic, and indirect in the way they present an opposing point of view.

The intention is to maintain a respectful environment and to exhibit proper social behavior. This acceptance of the manager's power is reflected by some Latinos' willingness to follow orders without resistance and by an obedient, somewhat submissive attitude at work (Zbar 2002a). Working under the assumption that the supervisor has all the answers, Latino employees will avoid contradicting a supervisor and will attempt to deliver even though they may view a task as difficult or impossible to do (Deforest 1994). Any judgment or friction in the relationship would be disruptive of harmony or be seen as an attempt to supersede the manager's authority. It is not unusual to hear a Latino say, "I don't understand management decisions, but I am a *good corporate soldier.*" Therefore, he will execute these orders somewhat blindly. His idea is that management knows better than he does. That is why they are "up there."

Sometimes Latino employees will be reluctant to express their ideas or opinions verbally. This does not necessarily mean that they do not have an opinion. In these cases, observation of their nonverbal communication (body language) will give cues to their views regarding a subject (Sosa 1999). An employee may lower his head, either in acceptance of the opinions of the supervisor or as a way to hide his own opinion and not have to disclose it. He may also prefer to have some private time to put his thoughts in order before coming back to the manager with a suggestion. The goal of this attitude is to be respectful, diplomatic, and careful in maintaining quality in the interaction (Kenig 2002). Being on good terms with the supervisor is a priority even if it implies not expressing oneself. This not only results from the deeply ingrained respect for others but is also a way to protect oneself. In those cases, a Latino will let others take the lead in whistle-blowing or publicly presenting a dissenting point of view. In the absence of verbalization of an opposing opinion, the mainstream manager may only notice dissent if he or she sees the employee procrastinating in performing the task or hears informal comments in the office. It may be a good idea for a mainstream manager to be direct in asking a Latino employee if he or she has a different point of view. In many cases, this is the signal that it is safe to speak and that the manager will not resent a dissenting opinion.

As discussed in Chapter 7, Latinos generally respond with loyalty to the employer as gratitude for the opportunities they have been given within the organization. There will not be a better representative or more grateful individual in the company. These individuals are not easily lured by others who try to tempt them to leave the company and work elsewhere. How can they leave someone who has been so good to them? Latino employees will say after long years of service, "*Aquí me salieron los dientes*"—"I grew my teeth in this company," which implies that they were very young when they joined. A Latino does not like to be misjudged as ungrateful. In fact, a Latino may let the manager or the human resources department know that she has been approached by a competitor but is not leaving the company. Latinos generally feel committed to return in hard work and productivity what they have received in trust and career advancement. When they find the right employer, they will generally stay there for a long time, working through the difficult as well as the good times. For Latinos, this long-term relationship with an employer may have more intrinsic value than salary or any potential career advancement with a new employer. Contrary to the apparent trend in the U.S., a Latino and his or her family will take much pride in having served many years in the same company. When observing the frequent changes of employer that are so common in the United States, Latinos may judge this "hopping around" behavior as due to instability, relationship problems, and an unhealthy sense of ambition.

A great need for emotional and financial stability may, at times, induce a Latino or Latina to accept less than desirable conditions at work. Such is the case of the recent immigrants, especially those who do not have their immigration papers in order. It is also the case of the Latino who cannot take the risk of losing the income the job represents while searching for a new one. The Latino saying, "*Un mal conocido es mejor que un bueno por conocer*"—"A known evil is better than an unknown good"—reflects the culture's views on changing supervisors and employers. In other words, a

Latino may prefer to keep a less than satisfactory job rather than risk the unknown.

Respect and appreciation are, as we have said in earlier chapters, great retention motivators for Latinos. Public forms of recognition may multiply the effects, because they allow others to see what these employees have been able to accomplish. A recognition letter for years of service or a birthday card from a supervisor may be proudly displayed in a Latino's cubicle as a major accomplishment and, in some cases, may be handed down to the children or grandchildren as a token of the parent's career. Having a good role model and close friendships within the work environment also establishes a Latino's sense of belonging to an organization and may compensate for a deteriorating environment and a stagnant career (Kras).

On the professional side, Latinos may be less demanding of benefits and compensation out of a sense of gratitude. They expect the manager to understand their situation and to take that into account with respect to personnel actions. They may see asking for a salary increase or demanding a specific bonus amount not as part of a negotiation but, rather, as a form of begging. Even when they do get up the courage to ask for more compensation, it is not without personal pain.

Latino employees are, as we have learned, usually assessed as individuals who work hard and show commitment to the task at hand (Gonzalez 2002). Their work ethic and responsibility can generally be counted on. One must remember that in most cases, Latinos have been taught to be obedient and to comply with tasks in order to honor family values such as responsibility. Thus, they give the best performance they are capable of and hope that their hard work can help them progress.

Some Latinos may judge other Latinos' sense of service as "servility." Such is the case of the administrative assistant who not only baby-sat for her boss, but also cared for their dogs and parrots at her own home when the boss and his family traveled.

The following vignette gives us a comparative view of how a Latino and a mainstream employee would see a potential job change.

VIGNETTE

അ Antonio, a native of Perú, moved to the U.S. a year ago after finishing an accounting degree. When he found a job with cellular phone company, he saw it as an opportunity to build his career.

His supervisor, Luis José, also Latino, helped Antonio understand some issues that were dealt with differently in mainstream culture from what he was used to back home. Antonio felt this had been to his advantage because Luis José understood Latinos. Antonio was grateful to Luis José and focused on his tasks, rendering very good performance in the accounting department of the company. He was good with numbers and information, tried his best, and was recognized for his work.

When Antonio had been on the job for 10 months, a relationship manager position opened up in the company, and senior management wanted to use it as an opportunity to develop an internal employee. Luis José proposed Antonio for the job, explaining his commitment and good performance. Dealing with clients was a new role, and Antonio was apprehensive because he had no previous exposure to that line of work. After several conversations with his boss, however, he decided to give it a try. Although he was reluctant, he did not verbalize this to Luis José.

Two months later, Antonio is called in for a conversation with Robert, his mainstream supervisor.

Robert: Hi, Antonio, come in and grab a seat. I have wanted to have a conversation with you for a while now.

Antonio: Thank you, Robert. It's good to have an opportunity to meet with you.

Robert: Well, Antonio, how have you been doing in this new job?

Antonio: OK, but not as well as I would want. When I came in, I had no experience with clients. I find that client service is a very demanding job. Every call is a surprisingly new event.

Robert: That's true. Clients want quality service for their money, and they are generally tough on their providers. Also, every case may be somewhat different.

Antonio: Yes, that's what I've noticed. Frankly, it's hard for me to return all the calls I receive, and when I do get to talk to a customer, I'm sometimes at a loss about the information they require.

Robert: Precisely, Antonio. That's what I've noticed also. Your performance is below our expectations. Your performance in the accounting department was very good, but it's being overshadowed by your current work. You come across as inexperienced and have not exhibited the resourcefulness that a client service person needs to have to fill that learning gap.

Antonio: I'm sorry to project that image, because I do care about my job and I'm trying hard, but it's difficult for me to cope with the responsibilities of this assignment.

Robert: As you well know, at the beginning I designated your most experienced peer to support you, and frankly there was a lot of feedback and hand-holding during the past two months. However, I see little improvement.

Antonio: I appreciate the support I have received from my colleagues, but I knew from the beginning this job was not for me.

Robert: What do you mean?

Antonio: Well . . . I don't know anything about the products we sell, how to service clients, or what to do in each of the cases. I don't even *like* what I'm doing now. I'm a numbers person. That's where I'm comfortable.

Robert: Do you mean you knew that you would not be successful in this job?

Antonio: Sure, I did.

Robert: Then why did you accept the transfer to this department?

Antonio: Well, I felt an obligation to do so because my previous supervisor, Luis José, told me I could do the job. He was so kind to me when I joined that he became a mentor for me. He said I could do this new job, and he is older, wiser, and more knowledgeable about the company than I am. He insisted it was good for my career, and I could not disregard his opinion. I owed him to at least try. Otherwise, I would have seemed ungrateful and uncooperative. I trusted he saw something in me that made him think I could do this job and that, with time, I would not let him down. He was acting in my best interests, but I have been unhappy all of the time I have been in this new role.

Robert: Why didn't you mention it?

Antonio: I am grateful to the company. I needed to continue trying. My cooperation was required, and I cannot let Luis José or the company down. All of you have been very good to me in my adaptation to this new country.

Cultural Pointers

- Luis José, the first supervisor, was trying to help Antonio progress in his career. To him, Antonio's commitment, loyalty, and effectiveness were more valuable than technical knowledge.

- Antonio was extremely grateful to Luis José, who had helped him adapt to this new environment, valued his work, and gave him advice. Luis José had become a mentor to Antonio.

- Antonio felt that if he told Luis José he was not interested in the client service job, he would be seen as lacking loyalty. He feared coming across as disrespectful and uncooperative. He was willing to try despite the fact that he did not feel comfortable with the transfer to the new area.

- Antonio did not feel he was doing a good job, but he did not approach anyone to discuss this. In typical Latino style, he kept on trying because he felt his effort was more important than the results obtained. He did not feel he could let the company down.

LATINOS AS COLLEAGUES

As we've discussed earlier, Latino work behavior tends to be guided by a sense of solidarity with coworkers, and interactions with colleagues are not limited to work-related matters. Latinos also pride themselves in "being there" for a peer who has a need outside of work and often socialize with colleagues.

Thus, it is not strange that a Latina will come to work with comments about personal matters, such as a fever one of the children had the night before, a discussion with her husband, or the good fortune of a sister who has received recognition for her hard work.

Personal Distance Latinos view relationships as extremely important, as we've discussed earlier. Latino coworkers are usually very open to others and seek to create empathy. They often turn to colleagues when they need advice, whether professional or personal, and they can be very open with their thoughts.

It is not uncommon to find that a Latino will easily disclose private matters early in a relationship, exhibiting substantial overlap between private life and the workplace (Warner 2002). There are only a few topics where full discretion is warranted. These tend to be identified with situations that may embarrass someone or subject an individual to judgment, as in the case of an alcoholic husband or a drug-addicted child. In these cases, among Latinos, judgment may be passed not only on the individual but on the whole family. A Latina may fear criticism from people who, if they knew, might feel free to ask how she could have married a man with a bad habit like drinking too much alcohol. Or they may accuse her of poor judgment, or ask how she did not see that her child was taking the wrong path, as if she were an irresponsible parent.

The mainstream culture tends to be characterized by a high sense of privacy. Individuals do not generally push themselves uninvited into someone else's life, nor do they share their own. If circumstances force them to interact personally, they usually do so only superficially. This is exemplified in many ways. On my (Francia's) first workday in the U.S., I got on the elevator and said a smiling good morning. Everyone lowered their eyes to look at their shoes. I felt I had done something wrong, so when I arrived at my floor, I made this comment to a colleague, who explained to me that this is a very private society. People on trains don't look at each other directly, nor do they engage in conversations with strangers in an elevator. I have learned to respect this difference, and now I have become a shoe expert: Every morning when I get into the elevator, I make sure to do as everyone else does and look at the floor, so as to not invade anyone's privacy.

For someone of Latino origin, it may be somewhat of a culture shock to come into an environment with such strong orientation to privacy. If the relationship with a peer is limited only to the professional, Latinos may feel they are not trusted or appreciated.

Professional Style Once a personal relationship with a colleague has been established, Latinos will invest time and effort in nurturing it. Sometimes this may mean having nonprofessional conversations during work time. Mainstream supervisors may view this behavior as a distraction from employees' assigned tasks. The best way for supervisors to approach this is to let the Latino employee know that they would like him or her to limit personal conversations at work. Then the Latino sense of respect and obedience will prevail. Latino coworkers will, however, continue to support one another in any possible way during work hours.

Latinos tend to be very cooperative with colleagues. Because they feel they have a duty toward the group, they will cooperate in terms of completing a task. Thus, they will usually be proficient in dealing with others in team settings; they enjoy being with their teammates and feel comfortable when working together.

The following vignette illustrates the different reactions a Latina and a mainstream person exhibit toward a coworker who may be having some personal problems.

VIGNETTE

〇〇 Mercedes, Jane, and Ana are coworkers in a clothing factory in New York. Mercedes and Ana are both Latinas. They immigrated to the U.S. with their families a few years ago. Jane is from the mainstream culture. She is empathetic to other cultures and welcomes diversity. She has worked with Latinos for a while, and although she does not understand some of their behaviors, she is respectful of their culture.

Mercedes arrives at work that morning with a concerned and distracted attitude. Both Ana and Jane notice this and discuss it among themselves.

Ana: Jane, look at Mercedes. Something is wrong with her. She has been acting weird all day, and she didn't even want to come along with me for coffee during the break. I don't know if it's something I did.

Jane: I don't think so, Ana. She's been the same with me. She is quiet and distracted today.

Ana: I'm going to go talk to her. I need to know what's going on.

Jane: Hold your horses, my friend. We need to give her some space. She will let us know what is troubling her when she is ready.

Ana: Jane, I love you dearly, but you just don't understand! You Americans see someone in trouble and you wait for a psychologist to come and help. We're not like that. We get involved. If she's in the river, we need to jump in with her. We'll find our way back together.

Jane: I feel uncomfortable with doing that. After all, it may be a private matter. What if she doesn't want to talk about it yet?

Ana: What do I care if she doesn't want to talk about it? If the shift supervisor notices a decrease in her production today, she's going to be in real trouble. Then she'll really have a lot to think about. I am just going to go over there and ask.

Jane: I want to help, too, but I am not sure this is what we should do. She may feel offended.

Ana: Well, then you can stay here and watch. That's why I'm a friend. I'd rather she hate me later, but I need to help her now, and I would do the same for you, even if you got offended.

(*Jane watches Ana make her move.*)

Ana: Mercedes, what's going on? You are really acting weird!

Mercedes: Nothing, Ana, I just have a lot on my mind today.

Ana: Well, my friend, you'd better shape up, because whatever it is, it's showing. If the shift supervisor notices how slow you're working today, you'll get in trouble, so don't give me that—tell me what's happening.

Mercedes: Well, Ana, I guess I have to talk to someone sooner or later. My husband, Juan, lost his job yesterday. You know we really need his salary, especially because our son is going to college shortly. I'm really worried. I mean, Juan didn't do anything wrong. You know he is a hardworking man, but the recession is bad and his factory is closing.

Ana: Don't worry, Mercedes; I know Juan. He'll get another job soon. Here's what you are going to do. You are going to give me half of the work you have for today, and Jane and I will help you do it. This way you can finish early and go home to help him think things through.

Mercedes: Thanks, my friend, I appreciate that. But you said Jane would help. How are you going to get her to do my work?

Ana: Oh, she's fine with it. She noticed how you were, we spoke about it, but she's waiting for you to be ready to tell her. Sometimes I don't get her. She's so polite she reminds me of an etiquette book. Anyway, she'll help. The three of us are close, and we'll support each other. Now let me hurry back to work before the supervisor thinks I'm gossiping with you again.

Cultural Pointers

- The feelings of concern and caring that Ana and Jane have for Mercedes are the same, regardless of their cultures.
- Jane prioritizes respect for Mercedes' privacy. Personal space is important, so she prefers to wait until Mercedes is ready to share her worries.
- Ana prioritizes her feelings and her need to support Mercedes. She is comfortable invading Mercedes' privacy if she can help Mercedes with her problems.
- Ana would rather risk a negative reaction from Mercedes than let her friend get into additional trouble due to her lack of productivity. She is willing to take that risk.
- Mercedes may not want to disclose her worries, because she may be afraid that others will feel her husband has done something wrong or is not competent, so she struggles with disclosing the news, even to people who are close to her.

The behavior of Latino supervisors and employees in the work environment may differ from the behavior exhibited by mainstream individuals. Less acculturated Latinos naturally exhibit many more Latino culture–based behaviors than those who have been in the U.S. for a number of years. The latter are likely to have become more acculturated and to have achieved academic degrees. Understanding these variations among Latinos and the differences in behavior between Latino and mainstream individuals can facilitate positive interaction between individuals from the two cultures and can promote a better work environment.

Specific Situations in the Work Environment

Latin American culture is diverse, upbeat, active, and often confusing when seen through the eyes of those from outside the region. Yet, this is the culture that strongly influences the way many Latinos in the U.S. act—at work and at play. In this chapter, we will explore typical Latino reactions to a variety of personnel actions: interviewing, hiring and firing, assessment and feedback, professional training and development, and sexual harassment.

INTERVIEWING

The immigrant Latino candidate comes into a job interview with questions that a mainstream person would not necessarily think of: Am I too old? Is my accent too heavy? Will my being a mother affect my chances for the job? Will I miss the opportunity because I didn't do an internship when I was going to school?

Many individuals who come from a different culture do not know whether what matters in their home country will necessarily be important in the U.S. They are concerned with being culturally correct. Thus, it is not uncommon that they should find opportunities in the interview to justify what they consider their flaws. They may say to the interviewer, "I know that I am over 50, but I can still work well," or, "My parents did not allow me to work and study, but I did gain a lot of experience from life itself."

Although interviewees from any culture will try to respond to the interviewer's liking, Latinos will try especially hard to do so. For them, every encounter is an opportunity to establish a relationship and expand their network. They want to please the interviewer and create a good impression, independent of the result.

In contrast, mainstream individuals will most likely present themselves for what they are, not necessarily for what they think the interviewer is looking for. If one company does not like their profile, they will continue to search for the right job in another company.

More acculturated Latinos are likely to consciously control their behavior and limit disclosure during an interview. They may try to mold themselves into what they believe is a mainstream style of formality and distance if they think that is what is going to make them look good.

A trained interviewer may perceive such behavior and mistakenly view it as a lack of honesty. Probing is recommended to confirm whether that is really the case, or whether the candidate is just trying to make himself more suitable for what he believes are the requirements of the job. Most likely a Latino applicant will not perceive that she is being unfavorably judged. Why would she, when she is only trying her best?

Most Latinos prefer networking (with family and friends) and personal contact as a means of identifying interview opportunities, as opposed to indirect contacts via the Web or e-mail. Acculturated Latinos who are educated in U.S. schools tend to seek jobs on their own because in U.S. culture, this approach speaks highly of their initiative and independence.

Latinos, especially recent immigrants to the United States, may feel more comfortable getting written or verbal recommendations. After all, what can be more powerful than a reference from someone who knows them? They may identify opportunities on their own but will still use their network as a way of gaining an introduction to a company. This method is effective, and sometimes the person making the referral may even take on this task independently for the candidate. Mainstream managers should not be surprised to get a call from one of their Latino employees who has a cousin who recently arrived in this country and is looking for a job, asking if it is all right for the cousin to call.

Such is the case of the Latino father who phoned me (Francia), looking for a job for his son. He told me a few things he thought were important to catch my interest. I thought it was fine when he mentioned that his son was a good student; that was applicable. I was only mildly surprised to hear his second set of reasons why I should interview his son: He was a Boy Scout, enjoyed mountain climbing, and did not currently have a girlfriend. When the father then said that his son had been close to banking all his life, I figured he was back on track, but then the father added that this was because at one time he—the father—had worked in a bank.

If you asked this Latino father, he would likely say that it was appropriate for him to do the search on behalf of his son, and the son would likely agree. This father was, in his opinion, offering me a great candidate—not only a good student but also someone with a hobby that indicated he was not averse to risk-taking. He was also trying to point out that his son had values and principles, such as those taught to Boy Scouts. The fact that the son did not have a girlfriend implied that he could give the job his full commitment and would work hard. Although his son did not have work experience, the father felt the son had seen, in his own example, the image of honesty and responsibility expected in a banker. For a mainstream interviewer, this would probably have been a confusing experience; the interviewer would probably have been left wondering what any of this had to do with qualifications for the job opening.

This chapter addresses some of the crucial issues to consider when interviewing Latino candidates.

PERSONAL INFORMATION

Latinos do not have strict privacy rules, and thus they will likely be candid and will self-disclose, especially if the subject is not something that will embarrass them. Their intention is to reveal honesty and transparency, and to highlight what they think is important: insight into their character and personality.

So much personal disclosure may unfavorably impress a non-Latino interviewer, who is usually accustomed to more reserve. Thus, this candid attitude can get some Latino applicants into trouble, because they may be judged as too open, creating doubts about their discretion. I have heard mainstream managers refer to Latino candidates who are expressive and candid as being "all over the place" when describing their exaggerated body language and verbal expressions. A lot of what a person sells is self-image, so if applicants do not pass the image test, they may be excluded even if they are well qualified otherwise.

The interviewer may feel uncomfortable hearing some of the disclosures of Latino job applicants, but it is important that he or she understand that recent Latino immigrants may be unfamiliar with U.S. labor laws and may not know that there are restrictions on personal information. Among other things, Latinos may naively comment on their values and beliefs, family origin, number of children, age, and marital status. This reflects the importance they place on personal details as a way of giving the interviewer insight into their individual qualities, thus making them appear better suited for the position. Latinos may believe an interviewer cannot hire them without really knowing who they are. In my (Francia's) experience, putting aside the restrictions applicable in the U.S., failure to ask personal questions may be interpreted by the Latino interviewee as a lack of interest on the part of the organization. Thus, it may be wise for an interviewer to explain at the outset why the scope of personal questions will be limited.

In my years of interviewing, I have not encountered a single written rule defining what questions should be avoided in interviews in Latin America; almost everything is allowed. Personal details play an important role. I once met someone from a hiring agency in the Caribbean who indicated that he always asked about the person's place in the family's birth order. He said that he could tell how a candidate would perform depending on whether the applicant was the oldest, the youngest, or the middle child. Such a question would be totally unacceptable in the U.S.

Reference to family in Latin America can be important but is not a requisite, as the following anecdote illustrates. After completing an interview in Colombia, I left some time for the candidate to add additional information and to ask questions. This young man indicated that although he found the interview thorough, I had not asked about his family. I candidly explained that it was not our custom to ask about private matters but added that I would be willing to hear anything he had to say if he felt it was important for my decision making. I patiently listened to the description of his nuclear family and the explanation of his upbringing. This was his custom and a way of conveying to me his values and principles, which would certainly make him, in his own view, a better candidate. Later, when I discussed this with my colleagues in Colombia, they indicated that an inquiry about the family was generally a required question.

Closeness   For a Latino, personal space includes the group, not just the person (Crouch 2004). In an interview, Latinos may appear to be more comfortable with closer physical distance than mainstream candidates might be. They are more willing to let strangers into their lives, provided the setting is a structured one, such as an interview. When the meeting is between Latinos, even in the U.S., both parties seem to understand this unwritten etiquette.

As a Latino interviewer, I (Francia) feel more comfortable interviewing at a closer distance and may even sit in a chair next to the interviewee. During my years of interviewing in the United States, I have learned to alert the mainstream interviewee to the fact that I will be sitting next to him or her, something that I don't have to explain to a Latino or Latina. My idea is to have a nice conversation among "would-be friends" instead of a formal, distant dialogue. I have found that physical proximity works better for really getting to know the candidate, but I acknowledge that it can be intimidating for a non-Latino. Mainstream individuals may be uncomfortable with such proximity.

Individuals of almost any culture understand that a handshake is the customary way of greeting and saying goodbye in North America. Latinos know this and are generally responsive to this style. However, some Latino interviewers and interviewees may kiss on the cheek as a sign of closeness and welcoming if the candidate was referred by someone known to the interviewer or is a friend of the family.

I (Francia) can clearly recall my first interviewee in the U.S.—a young, mainstream college graduate who was referred by a colleague. After a 90-minute interview, I felt I knew a lot about her, and we had developed mutual empathy. She seemed capable and had an appealing style. Thus, following my home-country custom and feeling comfortable with her, I shook her hand and also kissed her on the cheek to say good-bye. This handshake coupled with a kiss on the cheek is a natural way of expressing a somewhat less formal goodbye or hello among Latinos. I immediately saw the job applicant back away and blush. I felt I had to excuse myself, so I explained that I had recently transferred from Latin America and that this was the customary way to say goodbye in my home country. Since then, I have been very careful to operate in ways that are expected from the mainstream perspective.

Educational Differences If the candidate is an immigrant, the interviewer may want to ask about the academic grading system in the country of origin. This will allow comparison with mainstream candidates. In Latin America, academic systems and tests are not necessarily equivalent to those of the U.S. In South America, for example, most grading systems are based on a 1-to-10 scale. Even if they cannot make the conversion, most candidates have an idea of the GPA system used in the U.S.

The scheduling of the academic year may be different as well, because summer in the U.S. is winter in South America. Therefore, school is over in December, not May or June. As a result, there may be an influx of South American candidates toward the beginning of the year and not so many during the summer.

Although the SAT and other tests are offered in some Latin American countries, other countries may not have systems in place to offer the SAT, GRE, or comparable tests. If such tests do exist, it is a good idea to obtain the scores before making any judgment about a candidate's overall placement.

As we've said earlier, education is very important to Latinos. Those who have the opportunity to study are generally responsive and disciplined about their schooling as a way of returning their parents' investment in their education.

Strengths and Shortcomings As candid as Latinos can be, they may seem to hold back information if they feel they are coming across as too critical or if the issue under discussion is one that would embarrass them or their families. This is especially true of immigrants and of individuals in Latin America, where assessing one's shortcomings is not typical. These job candidates are not necessarily trying to hide information; they are just having a hard time dealing with disclosure, because they do not want to be misjudged.

Public self-assessment is simply not typical in Latino culture. The candidate may have a good idea of his or her personal areas of weakness but may find it difficult to describe them or to provide examples.

If the interviewer explains to the job candidate that he or she is asking the question in order to ensure finding a good match for the job and to support the individual in her professional growth, the candidate may be more forthcoming in revealing a shortcoming she would like to correct in herself.

It is also possible that Latino job candidates may not be able to offer a great deal regarding performance reviews by their former supervisors back home, because such reviews were most likely infrequent or nonexistent, as a result of the avoidance of negative feedback in Latino culture.

Work Experience The story of a Latino's work experience may be somewhat different from what a mainstream interviewer is accustomed to. Some of the differences include the way in which applicants got their jobs, assessments from supervisors, number of employers, and years of service.

In the introduction to this chapter, we discussed how Latinos tend to get their jobs through relatives and friends. This is so customary that in my interviews throughout Latin America I (Francia) have stopped asking people how they got their jobs, although this is a question that has great importance in mainstream culture, where it signifies initiative and independence. Older generations of Latinos do not generally have a large number of informal jobs (like summer jobs) early in their careers. In Latin America, if a young person takes such a job, it might be interpreted as meaning that a parent is in need of financial support, or might be seen as a distraction from the young person's academic responsibilities. As a result, summer or part-time jobs have not been common. Today, members of the younger generations actively look for internships and summer opportunities just as mainstream students do, although there may still be some restrictions on the type of work that is considered acceptable, as well as a concern that it be worthy of the family name and the person's time. For example, someone from a middle or upper social-class background would not easily take a job at a fast-food chain. For Latinos, social status is important and such service jobs in Latin America are largely relegated to individuals with less education and lower social status.

In mainstream culture, individuals often have numerous jobs in their lifetime, moving around every few years. In contrast to mainstream résumés, which may describe a wide array of employers and experience, Latino résumés are likely to list only a limited number of jobs. As we've discussed earlier, if Latinos could have it their way, they would probably prefer lifetime employment with just one employer.

Timing and Pacing Latinos view time differently than mainstream individuals do. Although they will try to be punctual in arriving at an interview, Latinos may not always be on time. There will be excuses regarding traffic or getting lost on the way, or applicants may take it for granted that the interview was at "approximately" 9:00 A.M., meaning as close to that time as they can possibly make it.

On a related subject, a mainstream interviewer may perceive that an interview with a Latino is intense, long, and burdensome, because the candidate offers such lengthy responses. Latinos tend to paint pictures in their conversation, to digress into stories, and to wander off the subject. This may cause the interviewer to perceive a loss of focus and control. Whereas a mainstream candidate will likely describe a job as "administrative, including filing, phones and billing," a Latino would say something like, "Well, the role was administrative, but I was really the manager's right hand. It was not a simple administrative job because I practically ran the office. I had filing responsibilities, and, believe me, they needed that, because it was a mess when I arrived. You could not find anything there. Imagine that they filed chronologically and . . ." Thus, the few words needed to answer the question may be transformed, in the Latino style, into a long monologue. Some crispness in the interviewer's manner of questioning can guide the interviewee toward the style preferred in the session.

Reference to People Because Latino culture runs on relationships, Latino candidates will likely use any opportunity to mention by name their boss, mentor, colleagues, family, or someone who has influenced their lives. They will generally refer to these individuals as if the interviewer were familiar with them and will go on to talk about the type of experience they had together. This is not only a result of their focus on relationships but also reflects the fact that in their country of origin, the interviewer is likely to know the person they are referring to; the community is smaller and closely linked.

The following vignette exemplifies an extract from an interview with a Latino candidate.

VIGNETTE

෴ Mark Philips, of mainstream origin, is the branch manager of a community bank in New York. He faces the task of increasing business in a predominantly Latino neighborhood. He enjoys sharing with individuals of other cultures and worked in a Latino neighborhood for some time, but he has never left the U.S. He realizes that to be successful, he will need to bring in people who can relate well to Latinos and can speak Spanish. He advertised the client service position, and Juan Martínez, a recent immigrant from Central America, has responded with an interest in the job opening. Juan speaks English well and has related work experience, so he seems a suitable candidate for this position.

Mr. Mark Philips: Mr. Martínez, thanks for coming in. I'm glad you have an interest in our open job. I'm going to ask you some questions about your work experience.

Juan Martínez: Mr. Philips, I must first thank you for the courtesy of granting me this interview. It means a lot to me. See, I recently immigrated to the U.S. and must now find a job for my family's sake. It is my pleasure to respond to anything you need to know.

Mr. Philips: Fine. Did you have any jobs while you were in high school or going to college?

Juan: During my first year in college, I had a job at a local supermarket. A classmate, who also worked there, recommended me. But then a friend of my father's saw me carrying grocery bags during my first week and mentioned it to him. You know how it is in small countries! My dad was ashamed that his friend would think I had such a job because he had financial problems, so he asked me to quit.

Mr. Philips: I understand. How did you feel about that?

Juan: Well, I really had nothing to say about it. I lived at home and my father paid all my expenses, including my tuition, so I simply obeyed.

Mr. Philips: I see that you also had a job at a local bank.

Juan: Yes, I am very proud that I have never worked for anyone else. I got there fresh out of college and stayed for 14 years. They were like my family. My supervisor, Carlos Herrera, was like a father to me. He is well known in the community there, and I even asked him to be the godfather for my oldest boy. We grew close and he visited the family often.

Mr. Philips: I see. And how did you get that job?

Juan: Well, my uncle Antonio worked in that bank for 20 years. He recommended me. I got the chance to interview because the bank knew him and his work, and knew that the family values would be the same. After I got the job, I worked hard to never let him down, and I didn't. I was recognized on several occasions for my performance.

Mr. Philips: I'm glad to hear you did so well. Why do you think you would be a good acquisition for our bank?

Juan: I am a responsible man. I'm already 35 years old. I have always provided for Natalia, my wife of 12 years, and my two children. Nora is now 10 and Miguel is 8 years old. My parents brought me up to respect others and do a good job. My long stay in that bank shows that I am committed and stable and that I have good banking experience. My immigration papers are also in order. Believe me, Mr. Philips, if you hire me I will work hard and stay with you for a long time.

Mr. Philips: OK, Mr. Martínez, let's give it a try. Can you start next Monday?

Cultural Pointers

- Juan quit his job at the supermarket to meet family expectations. By doing this, he pleased his father and, in his father's view, saved the family's reputation.

- A classmate recommended Juan for his first job. Juan's uncle recommended him to the bank where he had previously worked. In both cases, the jobs were obtained through others' recommendations.

- Juan understands that his long stay at the bank is a sign of his loyalty to the organization.

- He established a close tie with his supervisor, Carlos Herrera, whom he came to consider as family, even asking him to be the godfather for his first child.

- He mentions his former supervisor by name, although the interviewer is unlikely to know him.

- Juan discloses personal information that is not requested by the interviewer. He expects this will give the interviewer examples of his honest, responsible, committed, hardworking, and stable behavior. He hopes to come across as loyal and hopes these traits will favorably impress Mr. Philips.

- Because Mr. Philips has worked at a Latino neighborhood, he knows what to expect, even though he is somewhat uncomfortable with the responses.
- Mr. Philips accepts that Juan's style is different from the mainstream, and, after giving it some thought, he recognizes that Juan will be a good acquisition because his behavior mirrors that of his clients.

HIRING AND FIRING

Accepting a Job Because Latinos seek to please others as a way of strengthening relationships, they may seem willing to tailor themselves to company requirements in order to get the job. A human resources colleague recently referred to this as an "immigration syndrome," whereby individuals are so grateful to find a job that will allow them to adapt to the new country, that they will do almost anything that is required.

As we've said earlier, Latinos may believe that their good performance will be noticed and rewarded in due time, or, as we would say, "*Deja que te conozcan*"—"Just let them get to know you"— so getting in the door is the most important objective. They believe that positive outcomes will follow if they work hard and are attentive to company needs.

In the case of recent immigrants, this may result from the urgency of guaranteeing a stable income to cover family needs, so they are often more willing to take whatever position is available, rather than wait for the job they would aspire to have. This does not necessarily reflect that they have no personal preference but, rather, that they are also trying to please others. Latinos do not necessarily place a strong focus on salary, because they don't want others to think their aspirations are motivated by greed. They want to be adequately compensated, but they believe that projecting a sense of strong ambition may be seen as inappropriate. In addition, because salaries in their country of origin are generally lower than U.S. salaries, Latinos find they are generally making substantially more money here. For these reasons, Latinos will usually accept the salary that is offered.

Before accepting a job offer, less acculturated Latinos will also want to consult with family members. More acculturated Latinos may not verbalize their desire for family approval but will still request family members' input before making a final decision. Latino candidates will also carefully consider issues that might not occur to a mainstream person, asking themselves questions such as, "Will I be able to fit in?" and "Is the manager known to be respectful?"

This contrasts with the approach of mainstream candidates, who tend to accept only a job that is in tune with their skills and aspirations and that provides opportunities for career development, satisfaction, and personal attainment. They will be careful to negotiate salary, benefits, and even working conditions.

The acceptance of my (Francia's) first job was a thoroughly discussed family matter; my parents were personally involved in ensuring that the schedule was adequate and that I was working with the right people. More than 20 years later, when I had an offer to transfer to the U.S. on an expatriate assignment, I repeated the same process, this time with my parents, husband, and teenage children. Together, we explored the advantages and disadvantages of this move, as well as how to make it happen. I needed their agreement before making up my mind. If they had disapproved of the move, I would have declined the offer.

In contrast, when many mainstream candidates are offered a job, they may rely more on their personal goals than on family approval when deciding on a job offer. Although they can consult with someone they trust, such as a spouse or a mentor, most likely they have already done their research on the company and have determined their interest in the job before the interview.

Being Fired Losing a job is a particularly painful experience for Latinos because of their expectation of being employed for many years by the same company. The loss involves emotional, financial, and cultural issues, such as separation from a close network of friends and loss of a protective environment. For mainstream individuals, in contrast, the results may be mostly financial or a personal sense of failure or of being badly treated, as they have not necessarily established closeness with the employer or colleagues.

Some Latinos may also interpret dismissal as a sign of flaws in their relationship with their boss or colleagues: "What did I do wrong?" "Did I offend someone?" "Did I not meet my boss's expectations?" "Did I fail my peers in any way?" Losing a job may be particularly difficult in terms of the blow to a Latino's self-confidence. Although they work hard, Latinos in the U.S. are judged only on results. As we have seen, however, among Latinos, the effort to do a task may have as much value as the result itself. Thus, a Latino may alternatively interpret a dismissal as a lack of gratitude and recognition of their efforts by the employer. A Latino or Latina may ask, "Doesn't the boss appreciate me?" "Doesn't my boss see how much I am struggling to please him?"

A dismissal may move Latinos to feel personal guilt and frustration for not having been successful in selling themselves well. A feeling of shame may affect the individual's image and that of the entire family. Thus, Latinos may feel a need to save face socially so that they are not perceived by society as incompetent or unsuccessful. One way to do this is to say that they quit instead of admitting that they were fired. This is commonly used as a dismissal option in Latin American countries. Another option is for the employee not to mention the dismissal until he or she finds another job. Employees may do this by indicating that they are on vacation or on a leave of absence, or that they have taken a sabbatical to decide what they want to do next.

In contrast, although mainstream individuals also perceive the loss of a job as an important negative event in their lives, they often regard it as a result of business issues rather than their own inability to meet expectations. This attitude may make it easier to recover and to consider the loss as an opportunity rather than as a tragedy. Also, as many mainstream individuals are used to changing employers and moving from one location to another, they may be less disturbed by the idea of changing jobs.

Latino managers probably struggle more with a dismissal decision than mainstream managers because they have also established ties with the exiting employee. For a Latino supervisor, dismissing an employee may imply giving up on someone. Some managers may perceive the decision to dismiss an employee as a result of personal failure in their selection or management of the employee. Living in such an empathetic culture, Latinos generally try to support those who need help and quickly become involved as guides in people's careers. When they let someone go, it is generally because the employee is beyond their help, which causes them a sense of frustration. They will often give employees many opportunities to show improvement, and they may tend to procrastinate when it comes to dismissing an employee. As a result, they may need to be coaxed to complete the dismissal process effectively and in a timely manner.

The only exception is when a Latino manager must let an employee go because of unethical behavior. In this case, the termination decision will be rather quick because of the nature of the offense. Latino managers will not delay a decision to dismiss someone if they have reason to believe the person has been unethical or if there has been a breach of trust.

If a violation is serious, news of the situation will probably become public. However, Latinos usually prefer to deal with such matters privately. In one of the companies I (Francia) worked for, there was an ongoing debate about whether it was better to dismiss such an employee quietly or make the dismissal public to let the community know that this behavior was not tolerated in the organization.

Even if an employee is fired privately, the company may suffer the effects of Latino peer solidarity. Take the case of a longtime employee in an operations area, whose mother had also worked in the organization. After many years of service in the company, the daughter committed fraud, and, once this was identified, she was quietly let go. Lawyers were involved, but the firing was kept private, except for the ex-employee's mother, who was called to inform her of her daughter's behavior. Other employees, not knowing the true reasons for her termination, felt that the organization was being unfair. In fact, rumors circulated that the employee had been forced to commit fraud because salaries were too low. The comments subsided only when managers offered explanations of the events surrounding the dismissal. The saying, "When space is not filled with information, it is then filled with rumors," holds true here.

The following vignette exemplifies the Latino attitude in a dismissal.

VIGNETTE

෧෧ Julio recently immigrated to the U.S. with his family. As a result of his commendable work experience in Latin America and his fluency in English, he found a job he enjoyed as chief accountant in a retail store. He is known by the vendors, liked by other employees, and recognized by his supervisors as doing a good job. However, because business has been slow, the company has informed him that his position is being eliminated. Julio is sharing the news with Maricarmen, his Latina wife.

Julio: Honey, what I am about to tell you is very painful for me. Something really terrible happened at the office today, something that I have never experienced before in my professional life. I was fired!

Maricarmen: I can't believe it, Julio. How did this happen?

Julio: Well, my boss says business is slow, and they no longer need an in-house accountant, so my job has been eliminated.

Maricarmen: That's not possible. You are such a good employee. How could they do that to you? How ungrateful of them after all the hard work you put in!

Julio: I am devastated. I feel I have failed you, my parents, my children, and myself. I thought I was doing the right things and progressing in my job. But look at me, now I am unemployed. A failure! What did I do wrong? I'm sure this job elimination thing is just an excuse. Could it have been my performance?

Maricarmen: I saw how hard you worked, honey. You really helped them straighten out their accounting problems, so I don't believe it was your performance.

Julio: Then maybe I did something wrong. I thought my boss and I had a good relationship, but apparently not. I just don't know how to explain it.

Maricarmen: I don't know how to explain it either, but I am really surprised he did this to us. After all, he knows us well and has even visited our home.

Julio: You should have seen him when he told me. I expected he would tell me how sorry he was to have to let me go, but he gave me a very professional and formal talk about business needs. I guess this is the way things are done here.

Maricarmen: It would have been very different with your supervisor back home, but right now we must focus on finding a new job for you.

Julio: No one is going to want to hire someone who has been fired. They will suspect I have done something wrong. I feel bad about myself, and my self-image has been damaged. This is going to haunt me forever.

Maricarmen: We'll try to see how we can work around that. You are a hardworking man, so something should come up. What I am most concerned about is what to tell our families and friends. They will wonder why you were let go. Our parents won't understand this thing about discontinuing a position. Accounting is a critical role in a company.

Julio: I know, and that's what hurts me the most. I have brought a dark cloud over the family name.

Maricarmen: Don't worry—it wasn't your fault. We'll find a way out.

Cultural Pointers

- Julio is devastated. For him, losing a job is a very traumatic event. It is more than the job—it is also a blow to his self-regard and his sense of his own record as an exemplary employee.

- Aside from having to face the financial loss, Julio and Maricarmen need to protect their social and community image. They fear embarrassment and accusations of bad judgment.

- Julio, not fully understanding that the dismissal was a business decision and not necessarily based on his performance, questions himself. His self-worth is hurt, and he feels he has done something wrong.
- Julio and Maricarmen, unlike mainstream individuals, would have expected the boss to consider the family situation in the decision-making process and to show a more caring attitude.

ASSESSMENT AND FEEDBACK

Latino parents, when referring to school grades, will not usually tell their children, "Son, you are unfocused and distracted. This is affecting your grades, so let's find a way to work with your shortcomings." Rather, they will say, "Son, getting good grades is important if you want to make something good of your life. Your mom and I always worked hard to get what we have. To get you back on track, from now on you will not watch any TV until you have done your homework." The problem is addressed through discipline and philosophical teaching, but there is no discussion of the shortcomings that have caused the problem. These Latino disciplinary methods are geared to teaching the correct behavior, but not necessarily to pointing out or dwelling on negative traits. In the Latino culture, it is important to do the right thing—whether you believe in it or not, whether you have the skills or not. If you simply try, you're halfway there.

Having grown up in a culture that accentuates the positive, some Latino supervisors may find it difficult to deliver negative feedback to subordinates. Wishing to avoid jeopardizing the relationship, the supervisor will tend to skirt negative issues in feedback sessions. Mainstream individuals may be more experienced at articulating assessments, identifying goals, and setting deadlines for improvement. A mainstream supervisor, however, should take extra care to consider that conversations among Latinos tend to be more diplomatic, more caring, and less open in expressing criticism, and this style is what Latinos will expect in a feedback session with a mainstream manager as well as with any other.

Latinos are generally optimistic and are hopeful that people will eventually change for the better. Therefore, Latino supervisors are likely to believe that an employee can overcome his or her shortcomings. They may feel an obligation to give the person every opportunity to allow for that turnaround, even if it means delaying imperative business decisions.

Latino supervisors may even question whether their employee's poor performance is a sign of a flaw in their own management effectiveness. In other words, Latinos may view a failing employee as a reflection of their own poor management and thus may attempt to justify their subordinates' performance. Recognition of a bad hire may speak badly of their professional judgment, so they may delay giving negative feedback until it is inevitable.

Latino supervisees, on the other hand, can be quite perplexed when they receive negative feedback. These employees may react strongly if the feedback session does not take shape in a way that the Latino can understand. For example, they may get emotional because they have not developed a thick skin for dealing with someone pointing out their weaknesses. Worse yet, they may have no reaction at all; there may be a look of disbelief, because they are not sure what is really going on and what it means. Mainstream supervisors need to check that the employee understands what is transpiring in the feedback session. Even if the employee accepts the feedback, he may feel it is unfair for the company and the supervisor to be so harsh with him despite his efforts.

In the next vignette, we explore the reaction of a Latino manager as she delivers negative feedback to an employee.

VIGNETTE

၄၁ The head chef in a well-known restaurant, Rosa Pérez, is a second-generation Latina who is known to be a good manager. She studied to be a chef in the U.S. and has received recognition for her skills. She supervises a group of cooks at a large hotel, where she consistently delivers good results and also takes good care of her staff. At work, she retains many cultural behaviors learned from her parents, and this is reflected in her decision-making style.

One of her cooks, Manuel Morales, a second-generation Latino, has been missing work and making mistakes in preparing the dishes that are recognized as his specialty. The general manager asks Rosa to deliver this negative feedback to Manuel. After struggling with the idea of such a session, Rosa calls Manuel into a meeting.

Rosa Pérez: How are you doing, Manuel?

Manuel Morales: It's been tough, Rosa.

Rosa: I've noticed. I imagine a divorce is a serious matter, and these must be difficult times for you.

Manuel: I have not been myself lately because this is a hard and slow process, but I know I'll get through it. By the way, I appreciate the care you have shown and the time you have given me to deal with my personal issues.

Rosa: I am glad to have been able to help, Manuel. I know this has been a nightmare for you, and I don't want to aggravate the situation, but the general manager has asked me to talk to you about your performance. You have previously been recognized for the quality of the dishes you prepared, but your work has deteriorated. You know that we work in a very sensitive business. There's no second chance to prepare a good meal for a guest. I know this is a bad time to give you this feedback, but I have no choice.

Manuel: Rosa, I am doing my best, but there are tons of reasons why my performance is not optimal, one of them being the poor quality of the vendor we are now using.

Rosa: We can certainly look into that, but I think you should also recognize how you are contributing to this situation.

Manuel: But how can you bring this point up now, when I need everyone's support?

Rosa: Believe me, I have struggled with this conversation myself. I did let the general manager know that you have a difficult personal situation. I have tried to protect you, but it has come to his attention, so it is now out of my hands.

Manuel: I admit that the divorce issue has kept me somewhat distracted, but I didn't think it was enough for you talk to me about it. You know I have always been recognized for my performance. I even won the service and the quality awards a couple of years ago. I know you value my dedication and hard work, and I would expect the company to do so as well.

Rosa: The company does care, Manuel, but service is service. I figured it would be less painful if I had the conversation with you instead of someone who doesn't know you well. Believe me, I often sit here and wonder if I could have done anything different to get you back on track—assign you a different role or give you a longer leave of absence. You know this hurts my performance as much as it does yours, so we must find a solution together. I'll give you time to think about it, and let's set a meeting for tomorrow to discuss an action plan.

Cultural Pointers

- Manuel candidly shares personal matters during his conversation with his supervisor, Rosa. Although in other cultures it may seem inappropriate to share that information, among Latinos sharing is a sign of caring.

- Rosa feels that protecting her employees is one of her responsibilities. She is frustrated because she was not able to keep this situation from the general manager.

- The only reason Rosa is giving Manuel this negative feedback is that she was asked to do so by the general manager. If she had her way, she would give Manuel as much time as he needs to recuperate from his divorce and the effect that it is having on his performance.

- Manuel expects the company and his supervisor to tolerate and protect him in a time of need because of his history of good performance.

- Although Rosa was educated in the U.S. and probably knows how to deliver feedback, her Latino upbringing makes her struggle. Therefore, she procrastinates. She provides feedback gently, in order to protect the relationship and the employee's feelings.
- Rosa feels that she is also being evaluated regarding the deterioration of Manuel's performance. She torments herself, wondering what she could have done differently.
- Feeling that she is part of the problem, she sets a date for herself and Manuel to find a solution together.

PROFESSIONAL DEVELOPMENT AND TRAINING

Latino parents tend to overemphasize the importance of education to their children because it represents opportunity. Latinos will say, "You can't be sure that you will win the lottery or find a pot of gold, so education is your passport to a stable and gratifying future." Latino children grow up seeing learning as something to appreciate and pursue.

As adults, especially at the early stages of their careers, many Latinos search for companies that offer high-quality training programs because they value the opportunity to further their education. In Latin America, some companies are highly recognized for their training programs, to the point that they may be referred to as "the school of banking," "the university of pharmaceuticals," or "the college of commerce." These companies' outstanding training programs reflect their concern for their employees' development, making them preferred employers for many job seekers. In Latin America, multinational companies are recognized for excelling in that role. They are the market innovators and often set the benchmark for other companies.

With that mindset, Latinos who have immigrated to the U.S. are likely to select a company that supports their academic aspirations. They hope the employer will recognize their potential and see them as a valuable investment. Latinos may interpret company-paid training as an implicit employment commitment; their logic is that if the company were planning to dismiss them, it would not invest in their education: How can they dismiss you if they have just paid to train you on a new computer system? However, U.S. companies sometimes need to make a dismissal decision despite the fact that the person recently completed a training program. In those cases, the Latino employee is perplexed at receiving two conflicting messages.

As we have said many times, Latinos usually develop a sense of loyalty to the company they work for, particularly one that invests in them. They may even struggle with the possibility of leaving an employer who has invested in their training. In fact, training has been reported to lower turnover among Latino managers (Dina 2003). As a result, training opportunities are among the top factors that make one job offer more appealing than another for a Latino and may even supersede salary, benefits, and recognition.

An important aspect to consider when discussing training in connection with Latinos is the level of their current skills vis-à-vis the U.S. market. Many immigrants are not adequately trained to fill jobs that may require operating modern or heavy machinery. Sometimes high-tech equipment is rare in their home countries, so they may never have been exposed to it. Thus, it is important for hiring managers to make sure that these employees take the required training promptly. The learning curve for second-generation Latino employees may be shorter because many already have knowledge of the job, especially because many professions in the U.S., such as real estate brokerage, require or recommend certification. For immigrant Latinos, the learning curve is probably longer and is likely to require specialized training to learn to do things the American way.

In some cases, language proficiency may also be a stumbling block. When English-language training is not given adequate attention, work-related injuries and deaths may increase. Therefore, companies with a large number of Latino employees would be wise, from both a safety and a regulatory perspective, to take extra care in training (even offering training in Spanish) and in translating work procedures into Spanish to ensure that Latino employees have full understanding of the processes.

The following Latino joke illustrates how critical knowledge of the language can be. It goes back to a time when smoking was not restricted in the U.S. as it is today, so cigarette vending machines were everywhere. A Latino visiting the U.S. tries to buy a pack of Marlboro cigarettes from a vending machine. He puts in the coin and requests the brand, but he is missing 10 cents. A button on the machine lights up with the word *Dime*. Now, in Spanish, *dime* means "Tell me," so the Latino gets close to the machine and says, "Marlboro." He imagines that the machine is asking what brand of cigarette he wants instead of indicating the amount of change still required. This story speaks to the care employers should take in making sure that Latinos understand instructions and safety features.

The following vignette illustrates the feelings Latinos have about training and how it can affect other work-related decisions.

VIGNETTE

৩৩ Teresa is a young, first-generation Latina who came to the U.S. to pursue a graduate degree. Because of her excellent performance in both academic and work environments, the company where she did her internship sponsored her work visa to stay in the U.S. She has now been employed in this company as a financial consultant for three years. Teresa is happy with her employer, but in this dialogue she is discussing a new job opportunity with a mainstream friend, Gina.

> *Teresa:* Gina, I want your advice on a possible move to another company. A large investment firm has offered me a job to head their financial department. This company has very high standards in hiring, so I'm lucky that they even considered me.
>
> *Gina:* And you have reason to feel proud, Teresa, because you have worked really hard through school and at your firm. Congratulations! So, when are you joining them?
>
> *Teresa:* Well, I am having second thoughts, and this is where I need

your help. My current employer has been so good to me. My current company paid for my licenses, sponsored my work visa, and have given me continuous training over the years. I feel I would be betraying them if I leave.

Gina: But why would you feel like this? You have been very dedicated and have achieved very good results. They've done well by you, and you've done well by them; it has been to your mutual advantage. This new position is a promotion for you, and most likely you will not get that with your current employer.

Teresa: I know the knowledge I've acquired is mine, but I can't help but feel that I would be taking with me something that belongs to them.

Gina: Come on, Teresa. I can understand your sense of loyalty, but you have reached a ceiling at your company. There's nowhere for you to go there. You need to move to a company where you can continue to grow and learn.

Teresa: That is my dilemma. I recognize what you say, but still, it bothers me. After all, they saw potential in me, trusted me, and prepared me to grow. They invested a lot of money in my education, which is a sign that they value me. They would not fire me after supporting me with so much training. Just last month the company sent me to Canada for additional leadership skills, and that was an expensive trip. How can I leave now? I owe them.

Gina: Well, Teresa, I can't tell you what to do, but do continue thinking about it. Your company probably won't show that same loyalty to you if their business priorities change, and then what good is your loyalty? You may not want to let this opportunity pass you by.

Teresa: Thanks, Gina. I will do some more thinking.

Cultural Pointers

➤ Teresa places more importance on what her current employer has done for her than on the potential opportunity that lies ahead.

- Gina is more realistic than Teresa and tries to give her friend a reality check by raising the possibility that her current employer may not be as loyal to her as she thinks.
- The company's educational investment in Teresa has created an increased sense of loyalty and ownership, while, at the same time, Teresa knows that a better opportunity awaits her with the new employer, so it is hard for her to decide what to do.

SEXUAL HARASSMENT

Elsa, a first-generation Latina, is working as a secretary in the marketing department of a large auto-manufacturing company. She comes to see Amelia, the head of human resources, to indicate that she would like to transfer to another area. She has been in this company for two years but is now working for a new manager who joined the unit just a month ago. When asked why she wants to make this change, Elsa looks uncomfortable. After a short pause, she says that she would like the opportunity to learn about another area. Amelia suspects that the new manager might be the real reason she is asking for the transfer. She closes her door, sits next to Elsa, and asks her to tell her what is really going on. Despite continuous probing, however, Elsa sticks to her story, and they conclude that they will look for that transfer opportunity. A couple of days later, Amelia finds Elsa crying in one of the restrooms. She takes Elsa back into her office. Only then, as Amelia persists in asking questions, does Elsa disclose that she can no longer handle her supervisor's inappropriate advances.

A Latino or Latina who is being sexually harassed may react differently from mainstream individuals. There are often two likely scenarios:

1. A Latino or Latina who is being sexually approached against his or her will would likely prefer to resolve the situation by quietly transferring to another department or quitting the job. This is perceived as a better option than filing a complaint. Such is Elsa's position. She does not want to expose herself to what a harassment

case may require of her, and she does not want to embarrass the supervisor, who is a person of power and authority. She also knows it will be her word against his, as nobody was present to witness his inappropriate behavior.

2. Another possible scenario is related to machismo and overprotective attitudes, whereby family members may become involved in confronting the alleged harasser. This will generally be done personally and discreetly but can potentially escalate.

When I (Francia) was starting my career in Latin America, a female relative and I coincidentally worked for different departments of the same company. During a social event, her supervisor made an inappropriate comment to her. He would have said it was "just a comment," but she was uncomfortable enough that she stayed away from work the following day. I knew that she had no reason to miss work, so I pushed her into telling me what was going on. Once I heard the comment, which was of a sexual nature, I asked her to take a second day off while I handled the problem, and I cautioned her not to mention anything to family members. The next day, I told this manager I needed to speak with him immediately and privately. Once in his office, I confronted him with the comment and told him I would go to the general manager if he did not facilitate a transfer for her. A week later, she was already working for someone else.

In this case, I decided to take matters into my own hands because I felt that, if another family member had gotten involved, things might have turned ugly. I felt it was my responsibility to protect my relative and also to keep other family members out of the situation. Knowing the organization, I could better control events. I did not care that the manager had a higher position in the hierarchy than I did; I was not concerned about the consequences of this confrontation for my relative or myself. My only goal was to protect her at any price. This is a common Latino reaction, where both of the possible scenarios were present. My relative tried to withdraw from the situation, while I confronted her harasser as my right and duty as a family member.

Established corporate guidelines may not necessarily give Latinos the sense of comfort they require in dealing with harassment. The corporate mainstream procedure involves filing a complaint, going through an investigation, and expecting disciplinary actions for the offender. This would be a personal embarrassment to a Latino. Even worse, the case might eventually become public knowledge, adding social shame, an even worse embarrassment for a Latino. Therefore, Latinos may prefer to try to escape the matter quietly, as Elsa did, instead of waiting for corrective actions. If a case like Elsa's were to occur in Latin America, preestablished corporate guidelines might not exist, or legislation to deal with harassment cases might be so new that procedures would not yet be in place. If a Latina immigrant, for example, has not yet been exposed to the mainstream way of dealing with sexual harassment, her behavior may continue to reflect practices in her home culture.

Given that Latinos, as a high-contact culture, are accustomed to close physical proximity with others, they may be less sensitive when it comes to identifying sexual harassment. In fact, it is not uncommon to hear a Latino working in the mainstream say, "I know we're in the U.S., and these people are obsessed with harassment, but we're Latinos, so let's hug and kiss anyway." Or they may say, "I hope you don't accuse me of harassing you if I say you look beautiful today." As a result, they may mistake a sexual advance for friendly—and expected—behavior, because they are accustomed to displays of affection and exchanges of flattering comments. Those of us who are accustomed to working in the U.S., and are aware of what a somewhat careless behavior may imply, are careful to curtail our expressions of warmth when individuals from another culture are present.

Latinos may also share jokes and make comments at work that might be considered inappropriate—and therefore constitute harassment—in the mainstream culture. Among Latinos, such joking behavior tends to occur despite the setting and regardless of gender. Latinas are faced with the dilemma of either "playing grown up" and remaining with the "boys" as they make these inappropriate comments, or acting offended and leaving, as the male colleagues continue with their jokes—of which the departing Latina is about to become the subject. This can be a hard call for a Latina. Most mainstream women would judge this behavior as inappropriate and might even lodge a complaint with management, but for a Latina, this is harder to do.

Despite their somewhat loose language, Latinos are taught at an early age to show chivalry and to refrain from using foul language in front of ladies. Thus, when they do talk in these ways in front of Latina colleagues, the women may take this to mean that they are being accepted as "one of the boys."

Latinas' high respect for authority may lead some of them to be more accepting of subtle sexual advances from authority figures, because they will initially think they are mistaken in imagining that there is something more than a work relationship going on. They may even examine their own behavior, thinking that maybe they are inadvertently promoting the situation in the way they dress or address the harasser.

The following vignette indicates an unintentional but inappropriate Latino behavior at work. It can certainly lead to misinterpretation of the person's intentions. This situation is exaggerated—it is unlikely that all of the following actions would occur at the same time—but it serves to illustrate multiple manifestations of Latino male behavior at once.

VIGNETTE

ᦂ After several years of working for a large global organization in Latin America, Fernando, considered an employee with high potential for development, has been invited to work as an expatriate in New York. He is unaware of the behavioral changes that he will need to make in order to adjust to the norms of the mainstream culture. The following vignette illustrates Fernando's first 30 minutes in his new job.

9:00 A.M.—Fernando steps off the elevator. He's been to the New York office several times before on business and for the interviews for this new job, and he feels he now knows the support staff. He is in a very happy mood as he begins his new responsibilities, so he winks an eye and blows a distant kiss to Sally, the receptionist, and says, "Love you, Sally," while she is talking with two older gentlemen who have come in for a meeting.

He then greets the two secretaries on the floor with kisses on both cheeks, thinking he is flattering them. He goes on to say, "Jane, you look great today," and, "Monica, that dress is just wonderful on you. I guess you wore it to welcome me! It will be a pleasure to work with such beautiful ladies." Jane and Monica look on in total shock.

9:05 A.M.—Lorraine, Fernando's assistant, having been duly kissed on both cheeks, follows him into his office to plan the day.

9:15 A.M.—After discussing the agenda, Fernando begins, "Lorraine, it's going to be great spending time with you. We must get to know each other better. Why don't we go for drinks tonight after work? I heard there is a great happy hour at the restaurant next door." For Lorraine, all this happens at an uncomfortably close personal distance. She manages to tell Fernando that she would rather keep work separate from personal life. As he is beginning to explain that this is work-related, Fernando gets a call from a colleague back home who wants to wish him good luck in his new assignment. Fernando thanks him and, on the speakerphone, starts to explain to the caller his encounter with the mainstream culture this morning, as George, a colleague who works on the same floor, is passing by. "Listen, Pablo, this morning in a very gringo style I went to a coffee shop to get that horrible American coffee, and there I heard this great joke. Let me tell you about it, so you can share it with the guys at work."

9:25 A.M.—Fernando walks into the human resources department in response to a request that he report to the office immediately. He is unaware that Human Resources has already received several reports regarding his inappropriate behavior. Assuming that the call is related to his new position, he smiles at the staffing manager and says, "Diana, I hope you have found for me a competent, young, good-looking female analyst."

Cultural Pointers

- Fernando may create potential liability for the company through his lack of knowledge of the norms of respect and formality in the mainstream workplace.
- The behavior exhibited by Fernando—greeting women with a kiss, inviting someone from the office out for drinks, and sharing jokes— would have gone unreported in the Latino culture, either because these actions were not interpreted as threatening or because of Fernando's position of authority.
- The situation results from a different view of what constitutes respect at work. For many Latinos, close proximity, jokes of a sexual nature, and flattery don't constitute disrespectful behavior. In fact, Latinos would not engage in behavior they thought was disrespectful. Family and personal image are very important to most Latinos, as judged by society.
- Fernando's intention is to be nice and to show closeness to his new coworkers. It is likely that he means no offense and has no ulterior motives in his behavior. However, it is inappropriate in a mainstream professional environment.

Conclusion

We call the United States home because this country welcomed us and expressed appreciation for our expertise. We have also found the opportunity to further develop professionally in the U.S. by working for prestigious organizations where we interact with a myriad of individuals in various roles, as employees, colleagues, managers, and mentors of future corporate leaders. We are only two out of the many thousands of Latinos who today are part of the American workplace.

Latinos are an extremely diverse population. Taking an elevator in an office building in downtown Miami, walking down the street in New York City, or interacting with service employees in Los Angeles, San Francisco, Houston, or Charlotte, it is likely that you will encounter one or several Latinos. Chances are that you may not be able to identify them as Latinos unless they are speaking Spanish. They may or may not look like you. However, physical differences are only one of the many characteristics of this group. Latinos also differ in other important ways, such as social status, education, and faith.

Many Latinos are bilingual and bicultural. We wrote this book to share our thoughts about the "why" and the "how" behind Latinos' professional actions and reactions, particularly those of immigrant Latinos. Certain aspects of the Latino cultural heritage continue to be present despite an individual's level of acculturation to the mainstream culture and regardless of the differences between our countries of origin in Latin America. That is what we hope we have communicated to you in this book—the values that we share, despite our colorful and wonderful differences. We hope we have succeeded in avoiding stereotyping Latino professional behavior because every person is truly a unique individual.

One of us recently met a 50-year-old white American professional who indicated she had not been exposed to anyone who looked different from her until she was 20 years old. Thirty years ago this might have been a common comment. Today, many Americans of different races and ethnicities find themselves dancing salsa, drinking margaritas, and taking conversational Spanish lessons. In both professional and social contexts, mainstream individuals are exposed to Latinos with much greater intensity and frequency than in the past. For some of you, Latinos may be supervisors, coworkers, or employees; for others, they may be friends or spouses, or they may be your children's classmates. It is exciting to think about what the work environment will look like 50 years from now, when one in four individuals in the nation will have Latino heritage.

The fact that you have taken the time to read this book says more about you, the reader, than it does about us, the authors. It speaks to your openness and curiosity for acknowledging and valuing this nation's diversity, to your commitment to developing the communication skills necessary to work with others who are not like you, and to your desire to be effective outside of your comfort zone. We hold you in very high regard.

—Nilda and Francia

Bibliography

Alcalay, Rina, Fabio Sabogal, and Joanne R. Gribble. 1992. "Profile of Latino Health and Implications for Health Education." *International Quarterly of Community Health Education* 12, no. 2: 151–62.

Althen, Gary. 2003. *American Ways: A Guide for Foreigners in the United States.* Yarmouth, ME: Intercultural Press.

Alvarez-Recio, Emilio. 1997. In *Latino Success,* edited by Augusto Doyle Failde and William Doyle. New York: Fireside Edition.

Anonymous. 2002. "Hispanic Workers' Death, Injuries Cause for Concern, OSHA Says." *Professional Safety* 47, no. 4.

Axtell, Roger E. 1991. *Gestures. The Do's and Taboos of Body Language Around the World.* New York: Wiley.

Bernstein, Robert, and Mike Bergman. 2003. Census Bureau Estimates. Hispanic Report CB03-100.

Bosch, Maria C. 2003. "El Ser y el Tener: Tiempos de Reflexión." www.angelfire.com/tn/tiempos/vida/texto19.html

Bureau of the Census. 2003. Estimates. Hispanic Report CB03-100.

Bureau of the Census. 2001. Population Projections Program, Projections of the Resident Population by Race, Hispanic Origin, and Nativity: *Middle Series,* 2050–2070. NP-T5-G.

Bureau of the Census. 2000. *Census Bureau Facts for Features,* CB00-FF.11, 11 September.

Bureau of the Census. 1993a. *We the American Hispanics.* Washington, DC: U.S. Government Printing Office.

Bureau of the Census. 1993b. *The Hispanic Population in the United States: March 1993. Current Population Reports,* Population Characteristics Series P20-475.

Canada. Statistics. 2003. http://www.statcan.ca/Daily/English/040322/d040322e.htm

Cattan, Peter. 1993. "The Diversity of Hispanics in the U.S. Workforce." *Monthly Labor Review* 16, no. 8: 3–16.

Chavarría, Jesús. 2003. "Hispanics Defy Homogeneous Stereotype." Corner Office. *Hispanic Business,* October.

Chong, Nilda. 2002. *The Latino Patient: A Cultural Guide for Health Care Providers.* Yarmouth, ME: Intercultural Press.

Coppola, Vincent. 2002. "VW Cultivates Latino Loyalty." *Adweek* 23, no. 39: 5.

Cresce, Arthur. 1992. "Hispanic Workforce Characteristics." In *Hispanics in the Workplace,* edited by S. B. Knouse, P. Rosenfeld, and A. L. Culbertson. Newbury Park, CA: Sage Publications.

Crouch, Ned. 2004. *Mexicans and Americans: Cracking the Cultural Code.* Yarmouth, ME: Nicholas Brealey.

Deforest, Mariah E. 1994. "Hispanic Staffers: Management and Motivation." *Long Term Care Management* 43, no. 3: 43.

Dina, Berta. 2003. "Bilingual Workers Ascend Management Ranks." *Nation's Restaurant News* 37, no. 11: 8–18.

Domino, George, and Alexandria Acosta. 1987. "The Relation of Acculturation and Values in Mexican Americans." *Hispanic Journal of Behavioral Sciences* 9, no. 2: 131–50.

Eckman, Molly, Antigone Kotsiopulos, and Marianne C. Bickle. 1997. "Store Patronage Behavior of Hispanic Versus Non-Hispanic Consumers: Comparative Analyses of Demographics, Psychographics, Store Attributes, and Information Sources." *Hispanic Journal of Behavioral Sciences* 19, no. 1: 69–83.

Edmonston, Barry, Sharon M. Lee, and Jeffrey S. Passel. 2002. "Recent Trends in Intermarriage and Immigration and Their Effects on the Future Racial Composition of the U.S. Population." In *The New Race Question: How the Census Counts Multiracial Individuals,* edited by J. Perlmann and M. Waters, pp. 227–55. New York: Russell Sage Foundation.

Elashmawi, Farid, and Phillip R. Harris. 2000. *Multicultural Management: 2000: Essential Cultural Insights for a Global Business Success.* Houston, TX: Gulf.

Fast, Julius. 1970. *Body Language.* New York: MJF Books.

Fears, Darryl. 2003. "Latinos or Hispanics?" *Washington Post.* www.msnbc.com/m/pt/printthis_main.asp?storyID=956803

Ferdman, Bernardo, and Angelica C. Cortes. 1992. "Culture and Identity Among Hispanic Managers in an Anglo Business." In *Hispanics in the Workplace,* edited by S. Knouse, P. Rosenfeld, and A. Culbertson, pp. 246–77. Newbury Park, CA: Sage Publications.

Fernández, John P. 1991. *Managing a Diverse Work Force: Regaining the Competitive Edge.* Lexington, MA: Lexington Books.

Ferraez, Jorge, and Raúl Ferraez. 2004. "Leadership, Ladies and Gentlemen, Leadership!" Publisher's Letter. *Latino Leaders,* February/March.

Fisher, Marla Jo. 2003. "Hermanas sin Límites: Margarita y Norma Jiménez Logran Altos Honores en la Universidad de Harvard." *Selecciones, Readers Digest,* October.

Flass, Rebecca. 2003. "Gallegos Gets Mission: Hispanic." *Adweek* 52, no. 49: 2.

Forston, Robert F., and Charles U. Larson. 1968. "The Dynamics of Space: An Experimental Study in Proxemic Behavior Among Latin Americans and North Americans." *Journal of Communication* 18: 109–16.

Galvan, Roberto A., and Richard Teschner. 1995. *The Dictionary of Chicano Spanish,* 2d ed. Lincolnwood, IL: National Textbook Company.

Garcia-Preto, Nydia. 1987. "Puerto Rican Families." In *Family Therapy with Ethnic Minorities,* edited by Man Keung Ho. Newbury Park, CA: Sage Publications.

Gardiner, Clinton H. 1975. *The Japanese and Peru, 1873–1973.* Albuquerque: University of New Mexico Press.

Gibson, Dirk C., and Christina E. Sanchez. 2003. "Tomorrow's Latino Practitioners: Profiles of Hispanic Public Relations Students." *Public Relations Quarterly* 47, no. 1: 31–35.

Gil, Lydia. 2003. "Author Finds Spanglish Catching On in U.S." *Hispanic Business.* www.hispanicbusiness.com/news/news_print.asp?id–12576

Gómez, David. 2004. "Hiring Hispanics." *Latino Leaders,* February/March.

Gomez, Christina. 2000. "The Continual Significance of Skin Color: An Exploratory Study of Latinos in the Northeast." *Hispanic Journal of Behavioral Sciences* 22, no. 1: 94–103.

González, Arturo. 2002. *Mexican Americans & the U.S. Economy: Quest for Buenos Dias.* Tucson: University of Arizona Press.

He, Wan. 2002. "The Older Foreign-Born Population of the United States: 2000." U.S. Census Bureau, *Current Population Reports,* Series P23-211. Washington, DC.: U.S. Government Printing Office.

Heaney, Christopher K. 1986. "A Bank Grows in Manhattan." *American Bankers Association Journal,* 78, no. 9: 35–38.

Herrera, Carlos R., Michael P. Stern, David Goff, Evangelina Villagomez, Ariel Pablos-Mendez, Richard Scribner, Paul Sorlie, Eric Backlund, and Norman J. Johnson. 1994. "Mortality Among Hispanics." *Journal of the American Medical Association,* 271, no. 16: 1237–40.

Hispanic Business. 2003. "100 Influentials." October.

Hispanic Business. 2003. "Atlanta Companies Partner with Target Latino." September.

HispanTelligence Report. 2003a. "U.S. Hispanic Consumers in Transition: A Descriptive Guide." *Hispanic Business.*

HispanTelligence Report. 2003b. "Homeownership Among Minorities." *Hispanic Business,* October.

HispanTelligence Report. 2003c. "Occupational Structure." *Hispanic Business,* September.

Hofstede, Geert. 1980. *Culture's Consequences: International Differences in Work-Related Values.* Beverly Hills, CA: Sage Publications.

Humphreys, Jeffrey M. 2004. *The Multicultural Economy 2004: America's Minority Buying Power.* Selig Center for Economic Growth, Terry College of Business, University of Georgia.

Kenig, Graciela. 2002. "Motivate Your Workforce." *Hispanic Trends,* Fall.

Kent, Mary M. 1997. *Generations of Diversity: Latinos in the United States.* Washington, DC: Population Reference Bureau.

Kikoski, John F., and Catherine Cano Kikoski. 1999. *Reflexive Communication in the Culturally Diverse Workplace.* Westport, CT: Quorum Books, Praeger Publishers.

Kleiman, Carol. 2002. "For Hispanic Workers, Family Always No. 1." *Chicago Tribune,* December 17.

Kochhar, Rakesh. 2004. *Latino Labor Report: 2003: Strong but Uneven Gains in Employment.* Washington, DC: Pew Hispanic Center.

Kotkin, Joel, and Thomas Tseng. 2002. *Rewarding Ambition: Latinos, Housing and the Future of California.* Pepperdine University, School of Public Policy, Davenport Institute, Malibu, CA; La Jolla Institute, Ontario, Canada; and Cultural Access Group, Inc., Los Angeles.

Kras, Eva S. 1995. *Management in Two Cultures.* Yarmouth, ME: Intercultural Press.

Leslie, Leigh A. 1993. "Families Fleeing War: The Case of Central Americans." *Marriage and Family Review* 19, nos. 1–2: 193–206.

Levene, Ricardo. 1937. In *A History of Argentina,* edited by William Spence Robertson. The Inter-American Historical Series. Chapel Hill: University of North Carolina Press.

Levin, Jeffrey. 1991. "Religious Involvement Among Hispanic and Black Mothers of Newborns." *Hispanic Journal of Behavioral Sciences* 13, no. 4: 436–47.

Levin, Jeffrey, and Kyriakos Markides. 1985. "Religion and Health in Mexican Americans." *Journal of Religious Health* 24, no. 1: 60–69.

Longman Dictionary of American English: Your Complete Guide to American English, 2d ed. 1997. White Plains, NY: Longman.

Lucas, Julie R., and Gerald L. Stone. 1994. "Acculturation and Competition Among Mexican Americans: A Reconceptualization." *Hispanic Journal of Behavioral Sciences* 16, no. 2: 129–42.

Marín, Gerardo, and Barbara Van Oss Marín. 1991. *Research with Hispanic Populations.* Applied Social Research Methods Series, Vol. 23. Thousand Oaks, CA: Sage Publications.

Mayo, Yolanda. 1997. "Machismo, Fatherhood and the Latino Family: Understanding the Concept." *Journal of Multicultural Social Work* 5, no. 1/2: 49–61.

Mendoza, Charles. 2002. *Hispanic Americans. Families & Family Life.* City News Publishing Company.

Moellmer, Andrew, Kusum Mundra, and Waldo Lopez. 2001. *Hispanic Underrepresentation in Managerial and Professional Occupations: Alternative Explanations and New Evidence from the Current Population Survey.* Mentor. The Tomas Rivera Policy Institute. The National Hispanic Employee Association. National Press Club, Washington, DC.

Moncada-Davidson, Lillian. 1996. "Understanding Success Among Central American Immigrant Students." *Latino Studies Journal* 7, no. 1: 3–33.

Morrison, Terri, James Conaway, and George Borden. 1994. *Kiss, Bow or Shake Hands.* Boston: Adams Media.

Muller, Roberto. 1997. In *Latino Success,* edited by Augusto Failde and William Doyle. New York: Fireside Edition.

Mundra, Kusum, Andrew Moellmer, and Waldo Lopez-Aqueres. 2003. "Investigating Hispanic Underrepresentation in Managerial and Professional Occupations." *Hispanic Journal of Behavioral Sciences* 25, no. 4: 513–29.

Murguia, Edward, and Edward Tellez. 1996. "Phenotype and Schooling Among Mexican Americans." *Sociology of Education* 69: 276–89.

National Society of Hispanic MBAs. 2004. www.nshmba.org/whoweare.asp

Niemann, Yolanda Flores, Andrea J. Romero, Jorge Arredondo, and Victor Rodríguez. 1999. "What Does It Mean to Be 'Mexican'? Social Construction of an Ethnic Identity." *Hispanic Journal of Behavioral Sciences* 21, no. 1: 47–60.

Noble, Judith, and Jaime Lacasa. 1991. The *Hispanic Way.* Chicago: Passport Books.

Oboler, Suzanne. 1992. "The Politics of Labeling: Latino/a Cultural Identities of Self and Others." *Latin American Perspectives* 19, no. 4: 18–27.

Office of Management and Budget. 1997. "Recommendations from the Interagency Committee for the Review of the Racial and Ethnic Standards to the

Office of Management and Budget Concerning Changes to the Standards for the Classification of Federal Data on Race and Ethnicity." *Federal Register,* 9 July, Part II, 36873–946.

Offman, Jose. 1997. In *Latino Success,* edited by Augusto Failde and William Doyle. New York: Fireside Editions.

Pablos-Mendez, Ariel. 1994. Letter to the Editor. *Journal of the American Medical Association* 272: 1237–38.

Padilla, Amado. 1980. "The Role of Cultural Awareness and Ethnic Loyalty in Acculturation." In *Acculturation: Theory, Models and Some New Findings,* edited by A. M. Padilla. Boulder, CO: Westview Press.

Perea, Anna, and Michael D. Slater. 1999. "Power Distance and Collectivist/Individualist Strategies in Alcohol Warnings: Effects by Gender and Ethnicity." *Journal of Health Communication* 4: 295–310.

Perez, William, and Amado M. Padilla. 2000. "Cultural Orientation Across Three Generations of Hispanic Adolescents." *Hispanic Journal of Behavioral Science* 22, no. 3: 390–98.

Plante, Thomas G., Gerdenio M. Manuel, Ana V. Menendez, and David Marcotte. "Coping with Stress Among Salvadoran Immigrants." *Hispanic Journal of Behavioral Sciences* 17, no. 4: 471–79.

Porter, Eduardo. 2003. "Census Forms Work Hard to Find Proper Way to Identify Hispanics." *Wall Street Journal,* January 21.

Porter, Eduardo. 2002. "U.S. Firms Increase Hispanic Management." *Wall Street Journal,* June 20.

Porter, Eduardo. 2001. "Pan-Latino Identity May Be on the Rise in the U.S., Independent of Country of Origin." *Wall Street Journal,* May 10.

Radelat, Ana. 2002. "SBA Chief Passes First-Year Test." *Hispanic Trends,* Fall 2002.

Ramírez, Roberto R., and G. Patricia de la Cruz. 2002. "The Hispanic Population in the United States: March 2002." *Current Population Reports,* P20-545, U.S. Census Bureau, Washington, DC.

Repak, Terry A. 1993. "Labor Market Experiences of Central American Migrants in Washington DC." *Migration World Magazine* 21, nos. 2–3: 17–21.

Rueschenberg, Eric, and Raymond Buriel. 1989. "Mexican American Family Function and Acculturation: A Family Systems Perspective." *Hispanic Journal of Behavioral Science* 11, no. 3: 232–44.

Sabogal, Fabio, Gerardo Marín, and Regina Otero-Sabogal. 1987. "Hispanic Familism and Acculturation: What Changes and What Doesn't?" *Hispanic Journal of Behavioral Sciences* 9, no. 4: 397–412.

Salgado de Snyder, V. Nelly. 1987. "The Role of Ethnic Loyalty Among Mexican Immigrant Women." *Hispanic Journal of Behavioral Sciences* 9, no. 3: 287–98.

Salgado de Snyder, V. Nelly, R. C. Cervantes, and Amado M. Padilla. 1990. "Migration and Post-Traumatic Stress Disorders: The Case of Mexicans and Central Americans in the United States." *Acta Psiquatrica y Psicologica de America Latina* 36, nos. 3–4: 137–45.

Sandlund, Chris. 1999. "The Enthusiast." *Success* 46, no. 4: 40–41.

Sarason, Yolanda, and Christine Koberg. 1994. "Hispanic Women Small Business Owners." *Hispanic Journal of Behavioral Sciences* 16, no. 3: 355–60.

Shuter, Robert. 1976. "Proxemics and Tactility in Latin America." *Journal of Communication* 26: 46–52.

Sosa, Lionel. 1999. *The Americano Dream*. New York: Penguin Group.

Sosa Monsreal, German. 2002. "El Balance Entre el Ser y el Tener." *La Revista Peninsular* 637, 5 January. www.larevista.com.mx/ed637/opi2.htm

Stanley Foundation. 1994. *Latinos, Global Change, and American Foreign Policy*. The Stanley Foundation, Musactine, IA, and The Tomás Rivera Center, Claremont, CA.

Stavans, Ilan. 2003. *Spanglish: The Making of a New American Language*. New York: Rayo.

Stewart, Edward C., and Milton J. Bennett. 1991. *American Cultural Patterns: A Cross-Cultural Perspective*. Yarmouth, ME: Intercultural Press.

Stoneman, Bill. 1997. "Spanish Unites Hispanic Americans." *American Demographics* 19, no. 12.

Suro, Roberto. 2003. *Remittance Senders and Receivers: Tracking the Transnational Channels*. Washington, DC: Pew Hispanic Center.

Suro, Roberto, Mollyann Brodie, Annie Steffenson, Jaime Valdes, and Rebecca Levin. 2002. *2002 National Survey of Latinos*. Washington, DC: Pew Hispanic Center; Menlo Park, CA: Henry J. Kaiser Family Foundation.

Suro, Roberto, and Jeffrey S. Passel. 2003. *The Rise of the Second Generation: Changing Patterns in Hispanic Population Growth*. Washington, DC: Pew Hispanic Center.

Teck, Bill, and Bill Cruz. 1998. *Official Spanglish Dictionary*. New York: Fireside.

Therrien, Melissa, and Roberto Ramírez. 2001. "Hispanic Population in the United States, 2001." *Current Population Surveys*, March.

Thomas-Breitfeld, Sean. 2003. "The Latino Workforce." *Statistical Brief No. 3*, August. Washington, DC: National Council of La Raza.

Ting-Toomey, Stella. 1999. *Communicating Across Cultures*. New York: Guilford Press.

Todd, Raphael. 2001. "Savvy Companies Build Bonds with Hispanic Employees." *Workforce* 8, no. 9: 19.

Triandis, Harry, Gerardo Marín, Judith Lisanksy, and Hector Betancourt. 1984.

"Simpatía as a Cultural Script of Hispanics." *Journal of Personality and Social Psychology* 47, no. 6: 1363–75.

Umaña-Taylor, Adriana J., and Mark A. Fine. 2001. "Methodological Implications of Grouping Latino Adolescents into One Collective Ethnic Group." *Hispanic Journal of Behavioral Sciences* 23, no. 4: 347–62.

Valdés, Isabel, and Ken Greenberg. 2000. "Acculturation Counts—A Look at the Hispanic Consumer." *Consumer Insight*, December.

Verdecia, Carlos. 2003. "What Really Matters." *Hispanic*, July/August.

Wallace, Steven P., and Elisa Linda Facio. 1987. "Moving Beyond Familism: Potential Contributions of Gerontological Theory to Studies of Chicano/Latino Aging." *Journal of Aging Studies* 1, no. 4: 337–54.

Wanning, Esther. 2003. *Culture Shock, USA*. Portland, OR: Graphic Arts Center Publishing Company.

Warner, Malcolm. 2002. *International Encyclopedia of Business and Management*, 2d ed. London: Thomson Learning.

Warner, Malcolm. 2000. *Regional Encyclopedia of Business and Management: Management in the Americas*. London: Thomson Learning.

Weisskirch, Robert S., and Sylvia Alatorre Alva. 2002. "Language Brokering and the Acculturation of Latino Children." *Hispanic Journal of Behavioral Sciences* 24, no. 3: 369–78.

Weaver, Charles N. 2002. "The Effects of Generational Status on the Work Attitudes of Mexican Americans." *Hispanic Journal of Behavioral Sciences* 24, no. 1: 63–73.

White, Sara, and Susan Maloney. 1990. "Promoting Healthy Diets and Active Lives to Hard-to-Reach Groups: Market Research Study." *Public Health Reports* 105, no. 3: 224–31.

Zbar, Jeffrey D. 2003. "Hispanic Shops Raise the Visibility Bar." *Advertising Age* 68, no. 46: 2.

Zbar, Jeffrey D. 2002a. "Hispanics 'Look Up to Authority.' But Still DTC Ad Efforts Lag." *Advertising*, May 27.

Zbar, Jeffrey. 2002b. *Pharmaceutical Industry Market Potential Hispanic Americans*. Chicago: Print Media Edition.

Zimmerman, Rick S., William A. Vega, Andres G. Gil, George J. Warheit, Eleni Apospori, and Frank Biafora. 1994. "Who Is Hispanic? Definitions and Their Consequences." *American Journal of Public Health* 84, no. 12: 1985–88.

About the Authors

Francia Baez

Francia has nearly 30 years of experience in financial management in Latin America, with a strong emphasis on business development covering sales, client relationships, financial products design, and marketing. For close to a decade, she has focused exclusively on human resources, where she has brought a business perspective. Based in South Florida, she currently deals with human resources issues for 20 Latin American countries within a global financial organization. A sociologist with graduate studies in urban and regional development, she also holds a certificate in human resources and is a registered corporate coach.

Nilda Chong

Nilda is a nationally recognized leader in culturally competent health care. Her expertise is in cultural competence with Latino patients and social marketing of health to Latino consumers. She has international experience as a consultant/trainer of trainers with the Pan American Health Organization and the World Health Organization, as well as over 20 years of clinical and public health experience in Latin America. She currently works for the nation's largest nonprofit health care organization as director of one of its institutes. Nilda holds a doctorate in public health with a multicultural health specialty from the University of California at Berkeley. She is the author of *The Latino Patient: A Cultural Guide for Health Care Providers* (Intercultural Press, 2002).

Index